The Art of Managing Up

The Art of Managing Up
A Step-by-Step Guide to Help YOU Become the CEO of Your Career

Nejat H. Abdurahman

©2024 All Rights Reserved. No portion of this book may be reproduced, stored in a retrieval system, or transmitted in any form or by any means—electronic, mechanical, photocopy, recording, scanning, or other—except for brief quotations in critical reviews or articles without the prior permission of the author.

Published by Game Changer Publishing

Paperback ISBN: 978-1-965653-00-5
Hardcover ISBN: 978-1-964811-99-4
Digital ISBN: 978-1-965653-01-2

www.GameChangerPublishing.com

Praise be to God, Al-Muqaddim.

Love, gratitude, and appreciation to Mama and Baba, my siblings, Anton, my friends, my community, and my readers.

Ubuntu

Read This First

Just to say thanks for buying and reading my book, I would like to give you a free strategy session with me, no strings attached!

Scan the QR Code here to schedule the strategy session:

The Art of Managing Up

A Step-by-Step Guide to Help YOU Become the CEO of Your Career

Nejat H. Abdurahman

www.GameChangerPublishing.com

Table of Contents

Introduction 1

Part I – Set The Foundation and Embark 11

    Chapter 1 – The Case for *Managing Up* 13

    Chapter 2 – Why People Fail to Manage Up 27

Part II – Build and Ascend 59

    Chapter 3 – Ownership 61

    Chapter 4 – Be Invaluable 73

    Chapter 5 – Mobilize Your Boss—Adopt and Align 83

    Chapter 6 – Create Your Own Luck—Be at the Right Place at the Right Time 95

    Chapter 7 – High-Impact Communication 105

    Chapter 8 – Develop Strong Support and a Network of Thought Partners 113

Conclusion 117

Gratitude 123

Introduction

My Story

It was August 31, 2009, and I was about seven thousand miles away from home, on a Peter Pan bus from Boston to Amherst. I was excited and nervous at the same time. I didn't know anybody in Amherst; my entire family (parents and siblings) was back in Addis Ababa. I was going to Amherst to pursue a higher education. I spent all 205 minutes on the bus from Boston to Amherst reflecting on how steep the path forward would be.

Growing up as one of nine children, I was the first in my family to pursue a university education. My dad and older siblings were involved in the family business, and my mom was a homemaker. Though I was immensely grateful for the opportunity and had the full support of my family, being the first presented its challenges. Learning to seek assistance and mentorship despite discomfort became a necessity—from navigating coursework during my undergraduate study to refining my resume post-graduation and identifying a career path.

And then, there I was on the bus, the first in my entire family to pursue a master's degree in the USA, miles away from home. This, I knew very well, was going to present its own challenges, from understanding the new culture to creating new connections and charting a career path. As the first member of the family to come to the U.S., I would have to build anew. I didn't have the luxury of a family or alumni connection at the companies I wanted to work with, nor did I have anyone to guide me on how to advance my career. All of my connections were back home. I was on my own.

I thought that if I am going to be in charge of my career and succeed here, it's going to be through my ability to learn and seek the support and guidance of the people I meet. I believed that as long as I worked hard and did an excellent job, I would make it.

But I was wrong.

The journey was tough. When I completed my MBA and joined the career force, I felt inadequate and perpetually behind. The pressure to seize every opportunity, combined with the fear of not being qualified or knowledgeable enough, intensified my stress. Even though I was doing excellent work, adding value, and contributing, deep down, I felt like an imposter. Whenever I get compliments for my work, I would undermine them by saying, "I could've done more," and "I was only doing my job." I had set high expectations for myself and didn't want to take credit for or celebrate small wins.

At my first job, four of the people who joined the company with me had fewer qualifications but were promoted to management within two years, while I was not even in the discussion. I didn't even have the courage to ask why. I was confused and didn't know what I was doing wrong or what I could do.

I was stuck in the same position for almost five years. Although I liked what I did and the learning curve was there at first, it flattened over time, and I felt like I was not growing professionally anymore. I had my fair share of frustrations. I had some brilliant ideas and suggestions for improvements at the company I worked with, but I didn't know how to influence leaders in the organization, so no one took my ideas seriously or implemented them. I knew I had to do something different.

See, I used to believe that as long as I got my work done, excelled, and made a positive impact in the organization, I would be recognized and appreciated. I expected that I would have a productive working relationship with my boss, that my boss and other senior leaders in the organization would recognize my achievements and value add, and that I didn't have to state the obvious. Duh! Great work speaks for itself, right?

But again, I was wrong.

I learned the hard way that I was missing the key ingredient to success—effectively managing up. I learned that *managing up* is not only necessary but also the key differentiator between those who advance in their careers and those who are left behind, between those who get to do what they like and those who don't.

I started doing things differently, which I will share later in this book, but even as I advanced in my career and transitioned into a management role, I recognized that there's more to being a great leader than just being a good manager to your direct reports. I realized that being a great leader includes *managing up* and across, which means working productively with your boss and other managers at your level as well as your higher-ups, influencing them and their decisions.

I started making small changes in how I led and how I talked about my work, and I started proactively learning not only from experience but also by reading books. Some of my mentors knew me, but others had no idea who I was. I considered authors to be mentors; I read a book a week and listened to as many lectures and lessons online as I could. The beauty of the world now is that, despite the drawbacks and cons of technology, we have access to people, thought leaders, and authors like never before. We can read books, pick someone's brain, and get the best tips, all from the comfort of our homes. And that is exactly what I did. I made authors and thought leaders my advisors and mentors.

I demystified the myths I believed, gained more confidence, learned new insights, and applied the steps I learned. After failing many times, my career started to take off, and I started feeling alive, collaborating more, and thriving while doing what I love. My boss and the company I worked for started to appreciate me and the value I added.

In October 2020, I quit my full-time, secure, and well-paid job and took the leap to start my own consulting company (N-BAC), which provides advisory and leadership development services. Since then, I have dedicated my time to running my firm, learning, creating an impact, doing research, developing leadership development courses, and training leaders and managers.

Even though I am a lifelong learner and always push myself out of my comfort zone and engage in programs to learn and grow, nothing has put me on such a steep learning curve as starting my own business. Not the intensive MBA program I took years back, not the years of sales and business development that taught me to be okay with rejection, and not the national sales trainer role I held. Nothing compares to the real-time experience I am getting and the person I am becoming as a result of starting and running a business.

As an entrepreneur, I thought *managing up* wouldn't be necessary, but to my surprise, I found that it is one of the key factors for success, even for entrepreneurs. The ability to influence the industry and industry peers and clients, demonstrate the value added, and demonstrate return on investment (ROI) with clients is key to helping an entrepreneur succeed.

There is a saying: "Knowing what you do not know is power." At different levels of my career, I learned that I did not know what *managing up* was and that my beliefs about it were mistaken. This cost me a lot, but each failure forced me to learn more and do more research. This allowed me to begin *managing up* effectively, and I am grateful for the impact this has had on my career.

I was able to chart a path for my career and discover and do what I truly love, which is helping leaders transform the way they lead. By no means am I saying that what I have done is extraordinary, but as someone who grew up in a small town, the first in my family to pursue education and travel overseas, going from someone who was insecure and had absolutely no idea how to make it, to helping hundreds of leaders across the world means one thing: I am on the path to fulfilling my potential and dreams. The younger me would be proud.

The steps I share in this book put me in charge of my career, and I believe they can help you, too, to effectively *manage up*, chart your own path, create the right environment to help you be the CEO of your career, do what you love, feel appreciated for what you do, and get value as much as you give.

We all face different challenges in life. We are all given different playgrounds to explore and different circumstances to start from. Being the first in my family to travel this path allowed me to learn the important lessons I share in this book. We all face different obstacles and challenging situations, but where we go depends on how much ownership we take, how strategically we work, and how much we are willing to learn.

I learned the concepts in this book because I had to live them to survive and thrive in my career and, in the last four years, to help my clients do the same. This book is not an academic paper; rather, it is a step-by-step guide of wisdom, advice, and practical insights you can apply immediately. The concepts are taken from my reading of those who have done much research in the area and who figured it out, and more importantly, from my personal experience.

My role has been to compile this simple guide that a professional who is interested in thriving can apply. It's a book I wish someone had handed me on that Peter Pan bus on my way to Amherst when I first came to the U.S., before my first job, or when I first transitioned into a management role. I share it with you in the hope that it saves you from the failures I went through and guides you to manage effectively. Some of the insights I share in this book may not work for you. I understand that what worked for me may not work for everyone, but my hope is that the general framework offered here in this book will help you to chart your own path.

Why I Wrote This Book

I first wrote the concepts in this book for a workshop for a group of leaders enrolled at N-BAC Academy. I was surprised to discover that the topic resonated with many leaders from different walks of life and in different stages of their careers. Groups and organizations started asking me to speak on this topic. Each time I presented a workshop, an online session, or spoke at a conference, the feedback was incredible. I got feedback from various professionals, including leaders who expressed interest in dealing with bad bosses, influencing decision-making within their organizations, addressing feelings of being unappreciated and undercompensated, convincing higher-ups to implement beneficial changes, and finding sponsors at work. The stories I heard from these people—who told me how helpful the session was and how they wanted more—encouraged me to write the book.

When I decided to write the book, I am not going to lie—I felt like an imposter and hesitated to write it. However, I was reminded of the wise words from the Irish author/philosopher specializing in organizational behavior and management, Charles Handy. During his speech at the Drucker Centennial Celebration, Handy said, "You don't write a book to teach; you write a book to learn."[1] I took that quote to heart and decided to write this book to synthesize what I had learned. I pride myself on being a continuous learner, and this topic of *managing up* is one I want to continuously learn about and improve. It's also one of the topics I hope to share with the world.

In this book, I share what *managing up* is, what *managing up* is not, why all employees need to *manage up*, what usually prevents people from *managing up*, and how professionals can effectively *manage up*. I share five insights that can be applied immediately through action items. Hundreds of authors have written on each topic, and you are invited to read their works to expand your understanding. My role here has been to present the most actionable insights that can be applied

---

[1] Charles Handy, "Charles Handy on Qualities of Vision and Leadership," YouTube video, 47:03, posted by "DruckerInst," February 4, 2010, https://www.youtube.com/watch?v=KrR-OUSCWjE.

immediately. This makes the book ideally suited for those who need step-by-step guidance in simple terms, along with explanations of the core fundamentals that don't change.

Though companies, leaders, and environments differ, this book provides the fundamentals of *managing up*, which can be applied by anyone at any stage of their career. I'm confident that the actionable insights in this book will help you transform yourself and your career. You will learn what *managing up* is—and what it isn't—and discover practical steps you can take to take charge of your career. So, welcome to this book!

How to Read This Book

This book is a step-by-step guide to help you *manage up* effectively and take charge of your career trajectory. By the end of the book, you will know what it means to effectively *manage up* and have actionable insights to create a productive working relationship with your boss, even if you have a micromanager or a bad boss. The book will also give you the insights and actions you need to be recognized, appreciated, and, most importantly, compensated for the value that you add to the organization and your boss. You will learn how to collaborate effectively with your boss and other leaders in the organization, develop sponsors, ensure that you are presented with opportunities that are right for you, influence decision-making, and inspire others even without a title.

In part one of the book, chapters one and two, we will discuss how you can set the foundation and embark on the journey to successfully and effectively *manage up*. The first two chapters of this book will address what *managing up* is and what it is not, and then we'll get into what stands in the way of effectively *managing up*. You'll get an opportunity to answer a few questions to see how you currently *manage up*, where you are stuck, and where you need more work.

Part two of the book, chapters three to eight, is all about taking action, building, and ascending. The chapters in part two present you with practical steps to *manage up* effectively. While it is advisable to read chapters one and two of this book in order, chapters three through eight cover the tactics, strategies, and actions that you can take. Feel free to skip to the chapter you want to start with first. Each chapter has insights, action items, and reflection questions.

To make the most of this book, I highly encourage you to take your time while reading and answering the reflective questions presented in each chapter. Use the spaces provided to jot down your reflections, and take the actions recommended in each section. As is with anything else, having an accountability partner and someone to read this book with and share best practices is advisable, so invite your colleagues and friends and make this a shared activity. It will pay off.

If you would like to be a part of the community of leaders who are reading this book, join the *Manage Up* Community. Scan the QR Code to download the workbook and join the community.

PART I

SET THE FOUNDATION AND EMBARK

CHAPTER 1

The Case for *Managing Up*

The CEO of a company I was working with asked for a meeting with me. It was not unusual for me to have a meeting with him since we had recurring meetings, but this specific meeting was special to me because I was reflecting on how much my department had accomplished and how much of an impact we had created in the organization. I'd been working as a corporate trainer for about a year and a half, and I was incredibly proud of all of the department's achievements. We had doubled our sales revenue, identified inefficiency in the operations process due to several department team member errors, and designed and conducted training that reduced these errors by 50%. We also created several training programs to ensure that the sales team was up to date on guidelines and upskilled on sales methodologies.

Everyone on the team was excited, so I went into the meeting with a lot of positive energy. I sat down, and we started talking about a few other things. Then, the CEO said, "Nejat, I am questioning the relevance of the training programs and wondering if the training department is generating enough return on investment to keep it going."

I was shocked. I'd seen all of the achievements and the impact we were making, and I thought the results spoke for themselves. At that moment, it became clear to me that I had failed to manage. I'd assumed that everyone else, including my boss and other executives, would see the results and impact as much as I did. I'd failed to realize that numbers and data don't speak for themselves and that these executives were too busy with their own work and departments to analyze them. I should have provided them with a regular summary of the numbers, ROI, and impact.

I asked him if he would be willing to schedule another meeting before making his final decision. Fortunately, he said yes, and I prepared a detailed presentation to go through all of the numbers, the changes that we'd made, and the impact that that department was creating. Thankfully, he was able to see the impact, and I was able to show him the ROI.

While I was happy that we'd gotten on the same page, I couldn't ignore how much I had failed to *manage up*. That was a big lesson for me. I thought the results would be evident to everyone, but they were not. What I thought would be a meeting where my boss and I would talk about my team's achievements, and he would tell me how much he appreciated my work, ended up being a conversation about whether to keep the department or not.

I wasn't surprised when many professionals told me that they resonate with this because we think that our results speak for themselves, as does the data. Failure to *manage up* can cost you your career. In other cases, it can cause you to lose out on well-deserved opportunities for promotion, which happened to one of my clients, "Amy."

Amy had been working at a company for five years. She was an individual contributor who ran the fundraising program and single-handedly managed fundraising initiatives and relationships with donors. She was able to raise $5 million in a very short time, a number unheard of for this specific nonprofit organization. In addition to that, she added value beyond her assigned tasks and created a detailed database of donors. She thought proactively about how to add value and make an impact.

However, every time Amy met with her boss—at least on the days that she didn't cancel the one-on-one meeting—her boss seemed not only not to recognize her achievements and wins but also asked her to do the things that she had already been doing proactively. Amy left these meetings feeling frustrated, misunderstood, unappreciated, unrecognized, and not really knowing what to do. It wasn't a surprise when the director role opened up—Amy didn't get the promotion she'd been expecting. This was the last straw that made Amy decide to find an opportunity outside of the organization.

Cases like Amy's are not rare. There are hundreds of stories like hers.

When we analyze situations like Amy's or mine, it makes us wonder why some people are recognized, appreciated, and sponsored by their boss and other executives in the company while others are passed over for opportunities, and the value they bring is not recognized as it should. On the other hand, there are stories where people who add value and have a productive working relationship with their boss get promoted, are presented with opportunities, and get raises.

While being competent and doing your job well is important, studies show that those who consistently move up the corporate ladder are those who *manage up* effectively. A study conducted by McKinsey & Company, a global management consulting firm, shows that *managing up* and across is about 50% more important for business success than managing subordinates and well over twice as important for career success. In this study, McKinsey & Company asked 1,200 senior marketing executives from 71 countries about their perceived business impact (contribution to revenue and profit growth), career success, and characteristics against 96 variables, including leadership behaviors, functional skills, personality traits, socio-demographic traits, and external factors such as their fit with the company.

They supplemented this research by analyzing existing 360 data on 7,429 marketing and non-marketing leaders, a total of 67,278 individual evaluations by leaders, bosses, peers, subordinates, and themselves. Ultimately, the study found that *managing up* and across is more important than managing subordinates for business success as well as for career success.

In another study, this one conducted by Ladders, a U.S.-based job search engine that provides career news, advice, and tools for senior-level jobs, 88% of high-earning professionals said that *managing up* means career success, with 81% stating that it's important for getting pay raises and 86% stating that it leads to promotion.

Managing up is not just necessary but vital in today's dynamic work environment. Professionals who demystify the concept of *managing up* and master this essential leadership skill will accelerate their careers, influence decision-making, and inspire others, even if they don't have a title. They will positively impact the wider business, fostering a more harmonious and productive work environment.

Manage up as if your career depends on it—because it does. Great employees do not leave the management of their careers to chance. They are proactive and *manage up* effectively. They do not brag or arrogantly share their achievements, and they definitely do not kiss the a**es of their bosses. There's an art to *managing up*, and the sooner that you realize what your skill level is in this area and proactively take steps to *manage up* effectively, the better you'll be to take charge of your career and grow.

What Is *Managing Up*?

The *Cambridge Dictionary* defines *managing up* as "Working in a way that makes your manager able to do their work effectively."

Harvard Business Review defines *managing up* as: "Being the most effective employee you can be, adding value to your boss and to your company."

My personal experience, as well as stories and cases from my clients, have made me realize that many professionals, leaders, and managers are adding value, but the value is not recognized. I know professionals who are adding and creating value and are the most effective people they can be, but they are passed over for opportunities or are not sponsored by their leaders. That is why I would like to add to the definition of *managing up*, and define it as:

> **Being the most effective employee you can be while adding value to your boss, your organization, and yourself.**

Managing up means adding value to your boss, your organizations, and yourself and taking proactive measures to create the right relationships and environment to ensure that the value you and your team are adding is recognized, valued, and compensated for.

> *It's not the value you add that counts; it's the value you add that is recognized that will make the difference.*

The reality is also that you can add a lot of value, but if that value is not recognized or appreciated because it doesn't align with what the organization is prioritizing, it's not going to add value to you and your career. So, it makes sense to always ask how much of that value is recognized by your boss and the leaders in your organization.

Why *Manage Up*?

When I had that meeting with my CEO, and he questioned not only the value that I was adding but also the value of my entire department, I felt a deep sense of failure, and I had no option but to *manage up*. In the case of my client Amy, she was passed over for a promotion, and that made her realize that she had failed to *manage up*. What about you? Why do you want to *manage up*?

The best way to start *managing up* is by digging deeper and understanding the *why*. As they say, when you know the why, the how becomes easier. There's probably a reason you're reading this book. Are you:

- Contributing significantly but not recognized?
- Adding value but not compensated well?

- Adding value to the organization, but it doesn't align with what others think you're adding?
- Not getting the promotion you thought you deserved?
- Being passed over for an opportunity you thought was the right fit for you?

The *why* is going to be different for each person, but if you're going to make the most of this book and learn to effectively *manage up*, you will need to start with that.

I encourage you to take the time to really think about why you want to *manage up*. While it's okay to start *managing up* to solve an existing problem, it is not the only reason people want to do it.

Here are some more reasons professionals want to *manage up*:

- You have a career goal that you've set, maybe for three years, five years, or ten years, that you want to achieve, and you're proactively thinking about what you can do now to get there.
- You want to advance your career, get promoted, or get a raise, or maybe you're moving to a different department or line of work to do what you really love to do.
- You would like to have sponsors and mentors who want to invest in you.
- You want to be able to work productively with your boss, who has different leadership and communication styles than you.
- You would like to influence decision-makers in your organization.

Managing up is about you being in charge of your career and actively working to get to where you want to be. For this reason, it is important that you reflect and write down your why. So, go ahead and jot down why you want to *manage up*. Use the reflection section below.

REFLECTIONS

---

1. WHY do I want to *manage up*?

_____

_____

_____

_____

_____

_____

2. Learning: What comes to mind when I think of *managing up*?

_____

_____

_____

_____

_____

_____

3. Curiosity: What am I curious about when it comes to *managing up*? What would *managing up* do to me and my career?

_____
_____
_____
_____
_____
_____

4. Impact: What would *managing up* do to me and my career?

_____
_____
_____
_____
_____
_____

How Effectively Do You *Manage Up*?

Before we get to the next section, I want you to take the *managing up* assessment. This assessment is designed for you to learn how effectively you are *managing up*—or maybe not. There's power in starting with knowing where you are. That way, you can take the steps you need to based on the *why* that you laid out earlier. (Note: The assessment scoring interpretation key is at the end of the book.)

———————————— ●●● ————————————

Managing Up **Assessment**

Great employees do not leave the management of their careers to chance; they are proactive and *manage up* effectively. They do not do it by bragging or arrogantly sharing their achievements, nor do they do it by kissing the a**es of their bosses. There is an art to *managing up*, and the sooner you realize where you are in your skill level and proactively take steps to *manage up* effectively, the better you will be able to take charge of your career and grow.

This *manage up* assessment is the first step on that journey. There are six core areas of *managing up*, and this assessment will give you an idea of where you are on the scale and provide details of your current weaknesses and strengths.

Instructions:

Answer the following questions on a scale of 1 to 5, where 1 is "Don't agree" and 5 is "Strongly agree." Add up the scores for each section as well as the sum of the total. Results are provided in the appendix at the end of this book.

Section 1

_____ 1. I do excellent work, and I believe the results speak for themselves.

_____ 2. It's my boss's job to pay attention and recognize the great work I do.

_____ 3. By actively *managing up*, I can slowly develop my boss into a better manager or leader.
_____ 4. I actively *manage up* by challenging decisions made by my boss.
_____ 5. I expect my boss to actively care about my career advancement.

Section 2

_____ 1. I find *managing up* to conflict with my value of being humble.
_____ 2. I sometimes doubt my achievements and feel like an imposter.
_____ 3. I find it difficult to talk about my accomplishments at work.
_____ 4. I care about what my peers think about my interactions with my boss.
_____ 5. *Managing up* sometimes feels like kissing the a**es of the boss/executives.

Section 3

_____ 1. My boss and I don't see eye to eye on many levels.
_____ 2. My boss doesn't seem to recognize how much value I add.
_____ 3. I am not compensated enough for the value I add to the organization.
_____ 4. I don't have sponsors at work.
_____ 5. I have been passed up for an opportunity I thought I was the right fit for.

Section 4

_____ 1. I do not know my communication style (I have not taken an assessment).
_____ 2. I don't know my boss's communication and leadership styles.
_____ 3. I mostly skip one-on-one meetings with my boss to save time for the actual work.
_____ 4 My boss sets the agenda for our one-on-one meetings.
_____ 5. I expect my boss to ask me for updates about my work as he/she needs to.

Section 5

_____ 1. Watercooler conversations are a great way to chat with coworkers.
_____ 2. I think it is a waste of time to attend meetings with other leaders and decision-makers in the organization unless it is relevant to the work I'm doing at the moment.
_____ 3. When I recognize my team for great work, I don't copy my boss or other leaders.
_____ 4. My boss and I rarely talk about wins and achievements; we talk about challenges to be solved and focus on what needs to be done.
_____ 5. I sometimes go above my boss's head to have my voice heard.

Section 6

_____ 1. My boss thinks I am a complainer and whiner when I talk about real challenges.
_____ 2. My boss sometimes ignores my emails/messages.

_____ 3. Suggestions I recommend are rarely implemented.
_____ 4. Other department leaders don't know what I've been up to at work.
_____ 5. I haven't had a coffee/networking meet-up with someone in the industry lately (within the last month).

• • •

How to Know If You Have Managed Up Well

There are a few things that you will recognize if you're effectively *managing up*. This is not an exhaustive list, but you will notice:

- The value you create and add to the organization is known and valued.
- Your strengths, loves, and passions are known in the organization.
- The executives and bosses that you work with already know what you're really good at.
- The things that you've achieved are not only known but recognized.
- Your excellence is recognized and rewarded.
- You are taking a proactive approach to your career, and you know what you want out of it and are strategically getting there.
- Your boss and other leaders in the organization sponsor you and present opportunities that are right for you.
- You have a productive working relationship with the managers in other departments and professionals in the industry.
- Ideas you suggest are well considered, if not implemented.

What *Managing Up* Is NOT

A student in one of my courses on *managing up* was really frustrated with her boss. She did not see eye to eye with him and did not think he had good leadership skills. Now, let's be honest; most of us can relate to that. As we were going through the course, she seemed to have an "aha" moment. "Now I get it," she said. "I really have to *manage up* and help my boss become a better manager." I had to pause and share what *managing up* is not. What my student mentioned is one example of what not to do. Some professionals think that by *managing up*, they will change their boss into a better manager or change how the executive leaders work.

Managing up is not supervising or overseeing your boss. *Managing up* is not going above your boss's head to have your voice heard. It's definitely not evaluating or judging your boss's management or leadership style. Let's be honest—you might already be thinking they do not have the best management style, but you know what? That's not your role to change their management or leadership style.

Most professionals would agree that they don't have the best leaders, and that is okay; the key is that there is a way to work with that boss to be able to actively *manage up* so you get to where you want to get, so that your value is recognized, so you create a productive work environment. It's not changing or growing your boss to become a better leader.

With that cleared up, let's move on to Chapter Two.

CHAPTER 2

Why People Fail to Manage Up

"Until you make the unconscious conscious, it will direct your life, and you will call it fate."
~ Carl Jung, Swiss psychiatrist and psychoanalyst

What Stands in the Way?

From my years of personal experience with my clients, I have identified several reasons why people do not manage-up well and what stands in their way. These reasons range from a lack of knowledge and awareness of the importance of *managing up* to a wrong definition of *managing up*, belief in some of the myths associated with *managing up*, and a lack of the right skills to *manage up* effectively.

I have categorized these into six core reasons why people don't *manage up well*. If you've taken the assessment provided in Chapter 1, it will give you an idea as to where you are on the scale of effectively *managing up*, detailing your current weaknesses and strengths. Actively *managing up* not only gives you agency but also a productive and a "win-win" environment that will contribute to the overall satisfaction you will feel at work.

Here are the six reasons people fail to *manage up*. In chapters 3 to 8, we will look at how you can effectively manage them, but first, it's important to know if any of these categories resonate with you.

I. Naïveté

The naive do not understand what *managing up* is, and they believe the myths associated with it. If you believe your excellent work will speak for itself, if you think your boss will pay attention and recognize the great work that you do without you proactively doing something about it, then you fall into this category.

It would be amazing if we all could be lucky enough to have great leaders and work for amazing organizations. Unfortunately, that is not the case. While a great leader or manager will make it a point to develop their team, others are simply too busy or do not see it as their active role. People in this category complain that they're stuck with a boss they don't like. They hate going to work, dread Mondays, and are happier on Fridays. They don't see eye to eye with their boss, and in best-case scenarios, they try to avoid any unnecessary interactions with them as much as possible. And in worst-case scenarios, they're afraid of being laid off. People in this category think *managing up* is "a**-kissing" the boss and their executives, and they don't want to do that.

Naïve people believe that by actively *managing up* they can slowly develop their boss into a better manager or leader. They expect their boss to actively care about their career advancement, and they believe that *managing up* is tooting one's own horn or bragging about one's accomplishments. People in this category believe that if they do their job well and with excellence, the raise, the recognition, and the promotion will follow immediately.

They don't see the need to actively create a productive working relationship with their boss. They don't see the need to showcase their achievements. They don't see the value of promoting their work and achievements. They think, *I will be a good employee, and good things will follow immediately.* The problem with this is that if one is lucky enough to find the right leader, this will work, but in most cases, it won't. Some bosses will abuse their power and even take credit for your work. Others are too busy to recognize your value add, and while you may not be fired, you will be forgotten for better opportunities or promotions.

REFLECTIONS

---

1. What gets in my way?

_____

_____

_____

_____

_____

_____

_____

2. Learning: Where in my career am I being naive and/or inept at *managing up*?

_____
_____
_____
_____
_____
_____
_____

3. Curiosity: What myths about *managing up* do I believe in, and how can I unlearn them?

_____
_____
_____
_____
_____
_____
_____

4. Moving On: I will take this action to ensure naïveté doesn't get in my way:

_____

_____

_____

_____

_____

_____

_____

II. Self-Erasure in the Name of Humility

Sara is an accomplished marketing lead at a tech firm. She defines herself and is very proud to be a very humble leader. She also prides herself on rarely taking credit for her achievements and downplaying them. Whenever people compliment her work, she says, "No, it's nothing. That's what I am here for. I've only done my work."

Humility is a virtue most of us hold dearly as a value. It's a tendency to share credit for success and appreciation for others' contributions. Now, that is a great virtue. However, there are definitely downsides to misunderstanding and misapplying humility at work. In his *Harvard Business Review* article titled *Three Ways Humility Can Undermine Your Leadership*, Tony Martinetti lists ways humility can undermine one's leadership. The one I want to emphasize is deflecting praise or giving all the credit to your team. Some professionals believe that deflecting praise or giving all the credit to their team members will motivate the team members and possibly brand them as someone who is selfless. Downplaying your achievements can have a detrimental effect. For instance, if you are always giving credit to others, you run the risk of being seen as someone who hasn't added a lot. When praised by your supervisors or someone else, if you always respond with, "Oh, it was nothing. I was just doing my job. I'm just lucky to have a great team," you effectively erase your critical role in the team's achievements. This consistent deflection not only diminishes your visibility but also inadvertently limits your political capital, which is essential for your future leadership opportunities and for cultivating the organizational influence necessary to help your team, whether it's in the form of access to budget or promotion opportunities for talented employees.

When you're seen as a successful and powerful force in the organization, you're far more likely to persuade others to create the impact you want, and you can ease the path for your ideas and the staff you care about. So, it's very important to have influence with the executives, managers, and leaders in your organization. This requires not only the right understanding and application of humility but also finding the balance between recognizing your team's involvement and hard work while still showcasing your own role.

There are two ineffective extremes on this. Some professionals always think about themselves, and whenever there's an achievement, they say, "I did it," they attribute the success to their hard work or contribution while completely ignoring their team. That's definitely a bad strategy.

On the other extreme are people who call themselves humble leaders or humble professionals. They completely erase their achievements and focus on spotlighting their team. That is a lose-win mentality, as they're so focused on elevating others that they forget themselves.

Great leaders strive for the right balance of confidence and correct application of humility in praising their team and recognizing all of their own hard work and input. They also highlight how their leadership created the desired result. So, next time you are recognized for leading a successful project, you can respond with, "Thank you. I'm proud of what we achieved. It was a collective effort, and I want to highlight my team members' innovative approach, which significantly contributed to our success." In this case, you're acknowledging your role in the achievement while also uplifting your team members' contributions, hitting the perfect balance.

Most of us struggle with admitting that we've contributed to our team's success. One of the best solutions I have found for this is to practice being humble while also healthily expressing your accomplishments. To help you do that, here is a powerful quote from Rick Warren's book *The Purpose Driven Life: What on Earth Am I Here For?*: "Humility is not thinking less of yourself; it's thinking about yourself less."

So, as a great leader, you want to have the right balance of confidence and humility. You think about the accomplishments that you've made while acknowledging your team's and others' contributions. You don't have to erase or completely dismiss your achievements. Strive for uplifting your team while still acknowledging your role in their success. That's the right balance.

REFLECTIONS

1. How am I erasing myself and my contributions in the name of humility?

_____
_____
_____
_____
_____
_____

2. Learning: Where in my career am I misapplying humility?

_____
_____
_____
_____
_____
_____
_____

3. Curiosity: What myths about humility do I believe in, and how can I unlearn them?

_____
_____
_____
_____
_____
_____
_____

4. Moving On: I will take this action to ensure that misapplied humility doesn't get in my way:

_____
_____
_____
_____
_____
_____
_____

III. Imposter Syndrome

I was the youngest person on my team, not to mention the only woman, for almost five years. It was uncomfortable, but I was handling it okay until I got promoted to manager. All of a sudden, I was insecure. I thought, *I am younger than the people I am leading and have less experience. I am also physically smaller than most of them* (as if that has anything to do with the work we were doing), *and I have been in the country for less time than they have* (again, as if that has anything to do with the work we were doing)... I thought nonstop about why I was not qualified to be the manager.

- ★ Was I qualified to lead?
  - o Of course, everyone has to learn to be better, but yes, I was qualified and absolutely committed to learning and learning fast.
- ★ Was I passionate about the work, and did I give it my all?
  - o Absolutely.
- ★ Did I care about excellence and have ideas to make a difference?
  - o Absolutely.
- ★ Did I know the ins and outs of the work that we did?
  - o Yes.

Despite all that, sometimes, the thoughts in my head made me believe otherwise. It was imposter syndrome, which affects everyone.

The term "impostor syndrome" was coined in 1978 by American psychologists Pauline Clance and Suzanne Imes in an article called "The Impostor Phenomenon in High Achieving Women: Dynamics and Therapeutics Intervention," published in *Psychotherapy Theory*

Research and Practice. The *Merriam-Webster Dictionary* defines imposter syndrome, originally called imposter phenomenon, as "a psychological condition that is characterized by persistent doubt concerning one's abilities or accomplishments accompanied by the fear of being exposed as a fraud despite evidence of one's ongoing success."

According to *Psychology Today,* 25–30% of high achievers may suffer from imposter syndrome and around 70% of adults may experience imposterism at least once in their lifetime.[2] Well, you might ask, what does imposter syndrome have to do with *managing up* and being in charge of your own career?

The answer is—a lot.

For one, those who experience imposter syndrome are most likely to believe that their successes came as a result of luck instead of their skill, work, or focus. People who are experiencing imposter syndrome are most likely not going to be proactive about showcasing their achievements and broadcasting their value and will believe that they do not deserve the raise or promotion they just missed out on. If you are feeling imposter syndrome, you're most likely going to think, *None of what I've done, none of what I have, is because of my hard work.* When you think that, forget about promoting yourself or showcasing your achievements; you're actually afraid of being found out. That is going to be detrimental to your success because you're not actively going to go for that promotion that you deserve or seek out opportunities that really align with your values. You also won't be confident when presented with opportunities.

---

[2] Psychology Today, "Imposter Syndrome," published September 7, 2018, https://www.psychologytoday.com/us/basics/imposter-syndrome.

According to that same *Psychology Today article,* imposter syndrome can stifle the potential for growth and meaning by preventing people from pursuing opportunities for growth at work, in relationships, and around in their hobbies.

Confronting imposter syndrome can help people grow and thrive. We will look at some strategies for effectively addressing this issue. As mentioned, about 70% of adults may experience this. So, if you're one of those 70%, we have some strategies for you in Part Two of this book to address that.

REFLECTIONS

1. How is imposter syndrome getting in my way?

_____

_____

_____

_____

_____

_____

_____

_____

2. Learning: Where in my career and in what situations do I feel like an imposter?

_____
_____
_____
_____
_____
_____
_____

3. Curiosity: What myths about *managing up* related to imposter syndrome do I believe in, and how can I unlearn them?

_____
_____
_____
_____
_____
_____
_____

4. Moving On: I will take this action to ensure that imposter syndrome doesn't get in my way:

_____

_____

_____

_____

_____

_____

_____

IV. Lack of the Right Relationships

The fourth thing that stands in the way of people *managing up* is not having the right relationships. You might've heard the adage: "It's not what you know, it's who you know."

Building a nurturing and supportive relationship at work is one of the most important things you can do for your career. Building the right relationships will help you collaborate more and be more productive. It allows you to learn from and share best practices with others. You will learn about more opportunities. Having the right relationships allows you to know and be known in the workspace and industry.

People who lack the right relationships are those who are focused solely on the job when they are at work; they have a clear boundary between work and outside life. They think *I'm just going to do my work.*

I'm not here to make friends. I'm going to stick to what is required of me and leave it here when I head out. Now, that is okay, and in fact, having a clear work-life boundary is helpful for our mental health and family life. However, if you intend to collaborate or advance your career, you will need to build relationships at work—not only with your team members but also with people in other departments, your boss, other leaders in the organization, and even professionals in your industry who work outside your company. To see if the lack of the right relationship is getting in your way, complete this short exercise and find out how your networking map is.

Look at the image below and, without looking at your phone or device, complete the three steps.

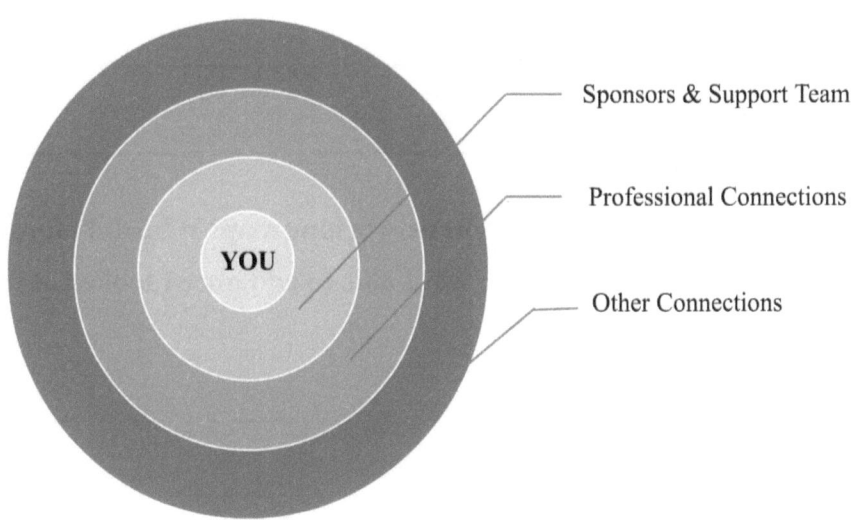

Step 1: list your sponsor and close support team in the first circle next to you. For this exercise, please use this definition of sponsor from the *Harvard Business Review* article: a sponsor is a senior employee who is invested in an employee's career growth and advancement. Sponsors

can be bosses, leaders of other business units, or even C-suite executives.

Step 2: In the second circle, list the people you would contact first for career help.

Step 3: In the third circle, list all other professional contacts and acquaintances.

Once done with these three steps, complete the same steps again, but this time, you are allowed to look at your phone.
How do you feel about what you see on your networking map? Use the questions below for reflections.

REFLECTIONS

1. How do I feel about my current networking map? Who did I forget the first time around, and who was I able to add once I looked at my phone/device?

_____

_____

_____

_____

_____

2. Learning: Do I have the right relationships I need to advance in my career? Do my connections align with my goals and career aspirations?

_____

_____

_____

_____

_____

_____

3. Curiosity: Do I have enough connections in each circle? What is the gap? Which relationships do I need to create, build, and nurture to effectively *manage up*?

_____

_____

_____

_____

_____

_____

4. Moving On: I will take these actions to ensure I build, develop, and nurture the relationships I need:

_____

_____

_____

_____

_____

_____

_____

V. Low-Impact Communication

The fifth thing that stands in the way of people *managing up* and taking charge of their careers is low-impact communication.

Do any of these statements sound familiar?

- "I've sent multiple emails, but I didn't really get the response that I wanted."
- "I've tried to suggest an improvement at work, but no one took my suggestions seriously or accepted or implemented my recommendation."

If the answer is yes, then you may have a low-impact communication style. If you are in a meeting with your executives or other stakeholders, and before you can get to your point, someone interrupts you, and you leave the meeting saying, "Gee, I was ready to present all of my findings, but I never got to do it," then you're practicing low-impact communication.

Low-impact communication ranges from the day-to-day communication that you have with your coworkers to even the water cooler conversations you have with your colleagues. It could be the emails you send to your team members, and it extends all the way to how you present in public, whether you're giving presentations at work or speaking at industry-wide events.

So, when it comes to key things that affect someone's advancement, communication is at the top of the list. In Part Two, we'll look at how to have impactful communication so you can effectively *manage up* and advance in your career.

REFLECTIONS

1. How is my communication getting in my way?

_____

_____

_____

_____

_____

_____

2. Learning: What are my strengths and weaknesses when it comes to communication?

_____
_____
_____
_____
_____
_____

3. Curiosity: What myths about communication do I believe in, and how can I unlearn them?

_____
_____
_____
_____
_____
_____

4. Moving On: I will take this action to ensure poor communication doesn't get in my way:

_____

_____

_____

_____

_____

_____

VI. Not Being at the Right Place at the Right Time

The sixth thing that prevents people from effectively *managing up* is not being at the right place at the right time. You're probably wondering, *How can I make sure that I'm at the right place at the right time? Isn't that luck?* No, people who are very proactive and have a win-win mentality are always looking for and creating opportunities to be at the right place at the right time. As author H. Jackson Brown Jr. said, "Opportunity dances with those who are already on the dance floor."

REFLECTIONS

1. How is not being at the right place at the right time getting in my way?

_____

_____

_____

_____

_____

2. Learning: Looking back at my career, how much of my success was because I was at the right place at the right time?

_____

_____

_____

_____

_____

3. Curiosity: What do I believe about luck, and how much influence do I have?

_____

_____

_____

_____

_____

_____

4. Moving On: I will take this action to ensure I am at the right place at the right time:

_____

_____

_____

_____

_____

_____

Before we move on to the next section, I want you to take a moment to reflect on this entire chapter. Look back at the assessment results and list what you think is standing in your way. Which of these six categories do you mostly find yourself in? Are you not *managing up* because of low-impact communication? Is it because you're not really finding yourself at the right place at the right time? Do you feel that you don't have the right relationships? Do you experience imposter syndrome? Are you erasing yourself and your contributions in the name of humility? Or are you not knowledgeable enough about *managing up* and unconsciously expecting your boss to do it for you?

Regardless of which of these beliefs is standing in your way, it's important to start by understanding and knowing where you are. The next chapters of this book will give you specific insights and action items that you can apply immediately so you can effectively *manage up* and achieve the results that you desire. Take some time to respond to the reflection questions provided in this chapter if you haven't done so already. Before we start talking about the actionable insights, though, let's talk about integrity.

Managing Up and Integrity

While *managing up* means effectively being in charge of your career and creating the right environment and relationships to add value to yourself, your boss, and your organization, there are cases where attempts to gain influence and *manage up* can go wrong. That is why I find it important to discuss *managing up* and integrity. A useful way to map and categorize the different ways to *manage up* and how to do so without losing integrity is to use a model offered by Kim James and Simon Baddeley.[3] James and Baddeley describe a four-sector model

---

[3] Kim James and Simon Baddeley, "Owl, Fox, Donkey or Sheep: Political Skills for Managers," *Managerial Psychology* 1, no. 2 (1978).

in their article "Owl, Fox, Donkey or Sheep: Political Skills for Managers," first published in 1978.

The authors depict the four groups of people using creatures representing certain qualities: a stubborn donkey, an innocent sheep, a clever fox, and a wise owl. The four-sector model is based on two axes: the skill a person possesses at reading an organization's politics and their predisposition to act with integrity or play psychological games.

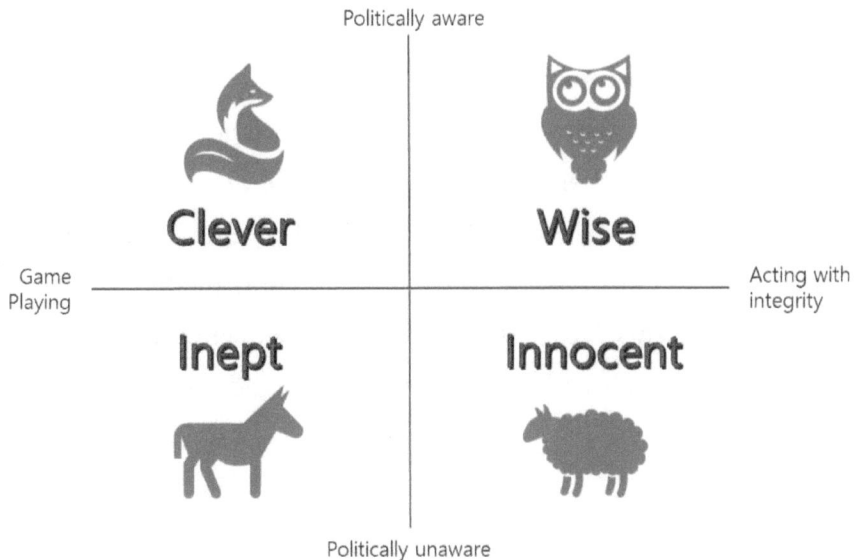

A person may adapt to different situations, so it's important to note here that these are behaviors and not fixed traits. This is critical because anyone can develop wise behavior by concentrating on being trained in specific dimensions of caring and reading and their combination. The first is the dimension of reading, which deals with the skill a person brings to their understanding of the external world. When it comes to *managing up*, it basically means understanding the organization that you're in, the people that you work with, and the external world, which includes the goals and priorities of your boss and the organization. The second dimension is that of caring, which describes the skill of managing your internal world.

The Inept

The first quadrant consists of people who are politically unaware and have low integrity: the inept. People in this quadrant are not skilled. They're unprincipled, they don't recognize direction, and they don't really appreciate political purpose. They're also interpersonally inept at making alliances and coalitions.

Ineptness includes the same inability to read political dimensions as innocence. But rather than internalizing the organization's needs, inept people, like clever people, are wholly self-oriented. The inept play psychological games in the organization that confirm all of their worst feelings about themselves and others. As a consequence, they often end up in a mess, which is bad for the organization and leads to bad results for them.

The Innocent

Innocent sheep, the second category, are good, decent people who have little or no influence and are often not powerful. They are prone to being taken advantage of, and their goodwill is often abused. Innocence, in this sense, is typified by blindness to power and other organizational issues and is used by people whose emphasis is on professional and managerial rationality. These people may view political skill as, if not actually contemptible, at least ethically compromising. They are unhappy about the whole business of politicking. They believe expert power and position power are the only legitimate sources of authority, and they are constantly surprised at the power that contradicts this.

The Clever

The third one is clever behavior. Clever behavior is typified by opportunism based on a shrewd understanding of how the system works. Clever behavior often achieves this without using the type of power innocents regard as essential. An innocent may observe with bewilderment that she knows nothing about the subject, yet everyone listens to her. People using clever behavior will set up situations so that the outcome meets their own needs. This is the low-integrity, high-political-skill quadrant, which may or may not coincide with what the organization needs. Those in this category only want to pursue their own goals, often at others' expense. They seek power and influence for their own sake and are willing to do whatever it takes to obtain them. As a result, principles and ethics are often disregarded in their pursuit of power and influence.

The Wise

The wise are those who have both integrity and influence. The wise, having internalized the organization's needs, are politically aware and act with integrity. They simultaneously pursue their goals as well as the organization's goals with integrity.

Now that we've established **the inept, the innocent, the clever, and the wise.**, let's look at how attempts to shift may go wrong. Let's look at this case: Among the innocent sheep, there may emerge some who become frustrated with their lack of influence and begin to adopt the unethical tactics and behaviors of cunning foxes to play the game, only to inadvertently become foxes themselves. They exchange their integrity for influence, and they allow themselves to sell their values when, in reality, it doesn't need to be one or the other. It's critical to understand how to become one of the wise—someone with both integrity and influence.

So, how can you be influential but with integrity? Be like the owls, which are well-placed to succeed because they are wise and highly observant.

Let's talk about this from a *managing up* perspective and consider the four quadrants that we're looking at in the visual.

The inept, those with low awareness and low integrity and low knowledge of *managing up*, are the ones who try to change their boss, don't like their work environment, don't like their job, are absolutely frustrated with everything, are a liability to the organization, and feel it's not the right environment for them. They do not see eye to eye with their boss. Worst-case scenario, they might get fired or quit their job.

The innocent ones are ethical and work with integrity, but they don't really have the knowledge of corporate politics or how to advance their careers. They don't have influence. These are the people who do their jobs with their heads down, providing excellent work and hoping that someone out there will recognize their contributions and promote them. They're humble, share with others, and highlight their coworkers. This type of person is amazing at what they do, and if they find the right manager, leader, boss, and organization, they might advance, but in most cases, they are likely going to be taken advantage of by those who seek power.

The third group consists of those with high cleverness but low integrity. These are the people who toot their own horns, who try to advance their careers at the expense of others. They might take credit for someone else's work, they might brag about themselves, and they might kiss their boss's ass. In the beginning, they might get what they want, but eventually, they'll be found out.

The goal is to be in the fourth quadrant of high integrity and high awareness. When you're in that quadrant, you're the wise owl, someone who is actively adding value to the organization. You are creating the right environment with your boss. You have internal awareness of who you are, your communication style, and your preferences. At the same time, you have awareness of who you work with, and you build that right relationship. You're advancing your career. You understand that *managing up* is a win-win: a win for you and a win for the organization. You're doing it in such a way that you advance your career and add value to the organization. This is a very helpful metric to look at because it gives you the vision of what this book is aiming to do: to help you move from the quadrant you're currently in into that of the wise owl who adds value to the organization but at the same time, adds value to yourself.

The goal is to be in charge of your career and create a win-win environment for everyone.

So far, we've looked at what *managing up* is, what *managing up* is not, and what stands in the way of success for most people. Now that you've identified why you want to *manage up* and have a deeper understanding of where you stand in terms of the six categories and where you fall in the metrics, the work is going to start. In part two of the book, we will discuss how to effectively *manage up* and explore actionable strategies you can take to be in charge of your career.

REFLECTIONS

1. Which quadrant do I mostly find myself in?

_____

_____

_____

_____

_____

_____

2. Learning: I have learned so far that…

_____

_____

_____

_____

_____

_____

3. Curiosity: I am curious about…

4. Moving On: I will take this action to be in the fourth quadrant (a wise owl)

PART II
BUILD AND ASCEND

CHAPTER 3

Ownership

Work is hard, and people are hard to deal with. If you're like most people, you want:

- Great working relationships with your boss and coworkers
- A work that you like and enjoy
- Productive days
- Promotion, getting a pay raise, and advancing your career

These things do not come to us or happen to us. These are things we create, nurture, and maintain.

One common trait of professionals who succeed on their own terms is ownership. These professionals know what they want and are willing to act ethically and with integrity to get it. They don't leave their fate or their dreams in the hands of other people. They know no one is coming to save them, and they don't assume that their boss is going to promote them or help them achieve their goals. They may hope that their manager is a great leader, but they do not rely on that for their career success. They prepare to tackle any challenges, including working with a not-so-ideal boss.

So, how can you take ownership of your career? Here are the steps you can take:

1. Define what success means to you and what your goals are.

"If you don't know where you're going, any road will take you there."
~ "Any Road," George Harrison

Take time to define what career success means to you. Define your ideal job and work environment. How can you make your work *work* for you? In this stage of your life and career, what are you looking for? People in different stages of their life might be looking for different things. Would that be more money or a higher salary? Or would it be a more diverse experience and exposure to different work types? Is it learning? Is it making an impact?

Now, think of the big picture and what you would like your career to look like ten years from now. How about five years from now? How about three years from now? And finally, how about in a year? Having a clear perspective about what career success means to you and how you want your career to serve you can help you set professional goals that align with your values and ambitions. When you have a clear vision of what you want to work with, the *how* will be easier.

Are you looking to make lifelong friends with those you meet at work? Do you want to work with people you can learn from? What type of people energize you? What type of work environment do you want? By having a clear vision for what you want out of your career, you can assume responsibility for your development and growth, encourage your team members to work toward a shared vision, and build a positive work environment.

With a vision in mind, you can identify areas for improvement in your current role and take specific steps to achieve your goal. By taking ownership of your career, you can build trust with your team, take the lead in your job role, and achieve success professionally and personally. Former Beatles member George Harrison famously wrote in his song "Any Road": *"If you don't know where you're going, any road will take you there."* The key takeaway from that is that you have to know where you're going, and you have to know what your goal is so you can start applying strategies and techniques to achieve that.

Goal and Intention Setting: Use This Page to Get Clarity on Your Career Goals

Use the box below to reflect on where you are now and where you would like to be. Your goal could be a list of skills you want to develop, leadership positions you would like to hold, or a salary you want to make. Be more descriptive of what you want your career to look, sound, and feel like 12 months from now, six months from now, and three months from now (include your role and salary).

My 1-year career goal is:	_____ _____ _____

My 6-month career goal is:	

My 3-month career goal is:	

2. Do a Knowledge Check

Identify where you are right now and what stands in your way, and address those challenges, specifically when it comes to *managing up*. When I was first promoted to management, I felt excited but nervous, as all the other sales team members were men who were older than me and had more experience.

Limiting beliefs flooded my mind. Without even realizing it, I started questioning if I could handle the job, listing all the reasons why I would fail. I thought, *I'm a tiny woman who's going to be managing men who are bigger than me*, as if size has anything to do with how we do our work, especially when it comes to managing people. Then I thought, *Wait, I wasn't born and raised here. Some of the people that I work with were born and raised in the U.S. How can I, a newcomer who's only been here for a few years, be a manager?* I started thinking of excuses as to why I was not fit to be a manager.

My self-doubt kept me from performing to my full potential. Thankfully, a wise mentor stopped me once and asked, "Nejat, why do you do what you do?" I didn't even blink. With a spark in my eyes, I told him everything that I believed about the work, how passionate I was about helping people, about the industry that I was in, and about training the team.

Then he said, "Why, then, are you thinking about yourself so much instead of about why you are doing what you are doing? When you think about yourself and why you can't or shouldn't be where you are, you are standing in your own way."

His wise words made me pause, and a light bulb switched on in my head. I realized I was thinking about myself a lot, and that was standing in my way.

See, when we think obsessively about why we don't belong where we are because we're not knowledgeable or big enough, we're not a man, we're not smart enough, or we're not this or that, we're taking energy and time away from what we could be. I took that to heart. That advice has always served me well.

Every time I think about why I should not be where I am or doing what I'm doing, I say to myself, *Stop thinking about yourself and focus on why you're doing what you're doing.* What about you? Go back to the assessment page and look at the results you got from *managing up*. What do they indicate? Where are you currently in the quadrant shared in chapter 2, and what stands in your way? As you set your goals, go back and reflect on your *why*.

Just as my mentor made me realize how I was unconsciously standing in my own way, I want you to reflect on and see how you may be standing in your own way. To paraphrase Carl Jung, until we make the unconscious conscious, it will direct our life, and we will call it fate.

You must first identify what is standing in your way before you can effectively address it.

3. Embrace *Managing Up*

One of the most useful mindsets to have when it comes to *managing up* is believing that it is a win-win. Many people struggle with this; most assume it is selfish to promote oneself, and others think organizations are selfish and have no intention of benefiting their employees.

Having a win-win mentality means believing that *managing up* is beneficial to all: to you and your career success, to the boss, and to the organization. Yes, it means having strong courage to advocate for one's career dreams and wants, but it also means having high levels of empathy and big-picture thinking, which means listening to what the boss and the organization want and striving to help them achieve their goals.

Recognize that *managing up* is a win-win. It is not manipulation. *Managing up* means you're adding value and making sure that the value is recognized. Just as you have career goals and you want to be recognized for your achievements, remember that your boss is also looking to grow their team members. Technically, your growth is the responsibility of your manager.

Just as you're interested in showing and adding value, your manager is interested in sponsoring and growing you. The key is to remember that this is a win-win situation, and you are also helping your boss. So, the first step is to be proactive in embracing *managing up*.

4. Unlearn the Myth of *Managing Up*

Most professionals are stuck because they believe the myths about *managing up*. Some professionals say, "I love doing the work that I do. I'm making an impact, but I don't want to toot my own horn. I don't want to brag about my accomplishments." They confuse legitimately sharing one's success with bragging. They naively believe that great work will speak for itself. Most professionals, especially women—particularly women of color and immigrant women—are not comfortable sharing their successes. That's okay—not everyone does—but it's something that we have to learn to do. It starts with recognizing the value that you're adding.

Zaria Pervez is the senior global social media manager at Duolingo. She states in one of her LinkedIn articles, "Whenever I explicitly say that I am the initial driving force behind Duolingo's success on social media, and I single-handedly built our community up to 5 million on TikTok, I inevitably receive angry messages telling me I'm pretentious and arrogant."

Those who believe the myth that sharing one's success is tooting one's own horn might send some nasty messages your way when you share your successes. The reality, though, is that great work does not speak for itself. Professionals who advance recognize this, and they know that naively believing work will speak for itself will only deter one's career advancement.

People of color, women, and especially junior talent often naively believe that their work will speak for itself. Unfortunately, great work, campaigns, numbers, and impressions don't talk. We do. But society might make you believe that. You are going to have to take an active step to unlearn the myth of *managing up* and be comfortable sharing your successes and stories.

5. Overcome Imposter Syndrome

Shellye Archambeau, in her book *Unapologetically Ambitious: Take Risks, Break Barriers, and Create Success on Your Own Terms*, defines imposter syndrome as a psychological phenomenon that causes you to see your insecurities as facts rather than opinions. It's characterized by a feeling of inadequacy, a belief that your success is undeserved, and a worry that you're a fraud. She says imposter syndrome is the combination of having skills without confidence and courage, and she offers five ways to overcome it:

I. Realize that you're in good company. Many professionals experience imposter syndrome just like you do.

II. Notice internalized self-doubt. Don't believe everything you think. Sometimes, you're going to have thoughts that are going to derail your career, so don't believe everything you think.

III. Believe the people who recognize your work and worth. Sometimes, when people tell you that you've done an amazing job, you think, *No, I was just lucky*. Don't believe that thought; instead, believe the person who's telling you that you've done an amazing job. Basically, believe the people who recognize your worth.

IV. When you're not feeling confident, adopt the "fake it till you make it" mentality.
V. If you're in a society that doesn't expect you to amount to much, remember that you can prove them wrong.

These five strategies will help you overcome imposter syndrome, but again, you need to continue doing the work.

6. Create Tools to Help You on the Journey

Imagine how great it would be if, whenever you were feeling insecure, someone reminded you how awesome you are, not just with words but with actual data. Well, that is what I call the **Wins/Achievements** document.

A **Wins/Achievements** document is a list of all of your wins (small or big), achievements, accomplished goals, praises you received, and kind words you received from the people you've impacted. I recommend that managers, leaders, and other professionals create such a document. It is important to note here that this document is not your resume. It's not your profile or portfolio, nor is it a document to be shared with your boss or anyone else. Rather, this is your personal document for yourself only.

This document can be updated weekly—or more frequently if you desire. You will come back to it often when you feel like an imposter and need support, a boost of morale, or a bit of motivation.

What to include in the wins/achievements document:
- All accomplishments and wins, both small and large—list everything, whether personal or career-related.

- The impact created at the project, department, or organizational level, such as the numbers you created or whether you increased sales revenue, met a project deadline, exceeded project expectations, exceeded client expectations, helped the company secure donors, etc.
- Praises and reviews: all congratulatory emails from your boss or anyone else telling you how much of an impact you created or how great of a job you did.

This document should be updated weekly, if not more often, to ensure you include every single win. When you start celebrating your accomplishments, no matter how small, you'll start to feel amazing.

This document will be useful in multiple ways. It will:

I. Help with your imposter syndrome. Whenever you feel like you're an imposter, you can open the document and see that you have added value and achieved goals. Seeing these tangible results will help you become more confident.

II. Help get you ready for any promotion or performance review discussions you may have. Looking at the document and reading your achievements before you have your performance review meeting with your boss will help you be aware of your accomplishments and the impact you have created and will give you tangible things to talk about.

III. Orient you to focus on results and impact. As they say, what we focus on grows. Constant focus on your achievements helps you find more ways to have a greater impact.

IV. Help with updating your resume and career advancement conversations.

V. Help you with your one-on-one meetings. Chapter 5 has a list of crucial conversations to have during your one-on-one meetings, and this document will help with that.
VI. Help you recognize your team's contribution so you can recognize them for their achievements.

With this tool handy for a confidence boost, it'll be easier to *manage up*.

Taking ownership of your career requires defining what success means to you and what your goals are, developing self-awareness, looking back at your trends to see what stands in your way, addressing those issues, and adopting the mindset that *managing up* is a win-win. It also requires the understanding that *managing up* is not manipulating your boss; it's not undeservedly getting something that is not meant for you. Instead, it is a win-win, creating an environment that is going to be conducive to work and putting you and your boss on the same page. Finally, you must create a wins/achievements document and not only update it on a continuous basis but read, read, and read it again until you've fully overcome imposter syndrome.

Wins/Achievements Document

Project-Level Impacts Created

Impact	Name of Project/ Department/Organization	Date

Accomplishments/Contributions

Accomplishment/ Contribution	How It Helped Your Colleagues, the Department, the Boss, or the Organization	Date

Praises and Reviews

Any congratulatory emails from your boss or anyone else telling you how much of an impact you created or how great of a job you've done.

Praise/Review	Received From	Date

CHAPTER 4

Be Invaluable

"Knowing yourself is the beginning of all wisdom."
~ Aristotle

The key to *managing up*, being the CEO of your career, advancing, and achieving all the goals that you have in your professional world starts with self-leadership, and the foundation of self-leadership is self-knowledge. Becoming invaluable to the organization requires you to lead yourself, have a deep understanding of your strengths and weaknesses, and actively work on becoming invaluable—or, in the words of Author Cal Newport, you must become so good that they can't ignore you.

More than ever, professionals are tasked with leading their careers, managing their resources, and ensuring that they remain relevant, thriving, and future-ready. Leading yourself and being aware of who you are, especially your strengths and weaknesses, will set you up for success.

So, how do you lead yourself?

A simple yet effective framework for self-leadership has three steps:

Step 1: Cultivate a deep understanding of who you aspire to be.

Step 2: Articulate it with clarity.

Step 3: Manage your energy and resources to create the best environment to help you get there.

To effectively *manage up* and add value to the organization and yourself, you have to start with a deep understanding of who you are. The steps provided here can be used by anyone, regardless of their career level, whether they're just starting out or are an advanced leader. I believe that successful professionals are always learning and always aspire to something greater. Now, how do you do this? By cultivating a deep understanding of who you are, self-knowledge gives you the clarity to understand reality and envision what is possible for you and where you can leave your mark.

So, what type of self-knowledge is worth exploring and reflecting on for self-leadership? And how does one go about exploring?

The first step is understanding your guiding principles and your strengths, including:

- Your values.
- Your *why*.
- Your true north.
- Where/when you shine.
- What your talents and gifts are.
- Which environments will bring out and spotlight your strengths.
- Your performance styles, especially when it comes to your leadership style, communication style, and interpersonal strengths.

In chapters 1 and 2, you've already completed the **Manage Up Assessment** and found out how effectively you're *managing up*; that's going to tell you where you stand, which areas you're strong in, and which areas you need to work on. You have also already taken steps to determine what stands in your way, and you've probably jotted down the areas that resonated with you. The next step is identifying your strengths and communication and leadership styles.

Identifying these characteristics is not only key to creating the right environment and relationship with your boss, but it will also help you identify the skills you have to hone to be invaluable to your boss, the organization, and the industry.

There are several assessment tools to consider to help you gain more self-knowledge, especially regarding your strengths and unique gifts. Here are four I recommend:

1. DISC

The DISC assessment is a valuable behavior-profiling system that educates users on recognizing and leveraging predictable communication patterns. Developed by Dr. William Moulton Marston, the DISC tool is highly regarded in behavior profiling and is backed by extensive research and validation. Whether you are part of a large corporation or a small business, the DISC provides accurate insights. It is a simple, practical, easy-to-remember, and universally applicable model. It focuses on individual patterns of external, observable behaviors and measures the intensity of characteristics using scales of directness and openness for each of the four styles: **Dominance, Influence, Steadiness, and Conscientious.**

The DISC model makes it easy to identify and understand our style, recognize and cognitively adapt to different styles, and develop a process to communicate more effectively with others. I recommend you take the assessment; you can find the link by scanning the QR code at the beginning of the book. The assessment report does an excellent job of telling you your tendencies, strengths, and weaknesses, what types of environments you need, how you might come across to others, and how you can align with other personalities/communication styles.

The main principle of DISC is that once you know your communication tendencies and style, you must then practice the platinum rule, which is to communicate with others the way they want to be communicated.

2. StrengthsFinder

The StrengthsFinder assessment, previously referred to as the Clifton StrengthsFinder, is an online tool designed to help people recognize their strengths and talents. This assessment evaluates consistent patterns of thinking, feeling, and behavior within 34 themes categorized into four domains: strategic thinking, relationship building, influencing, and executing. Upon finishing the assessment, users receive a detailed report outlining their top strengths and personalized descriptions.

3. StandOut

The StandOut assessment evaluates your alignment with nine roles and identifies your primary and secondary roles. These two key roles showcase your talents and abilities, reflecting how you naturally contribute to the world. By highlighting actions that leverage your unique strengths, StandOut enhances your performance. Your top two roles may differ from your self-perception, revealing how others perceive you. They pinpoint your consistent responses and behaviors, offering you a competitive advantage in the workplace. The report helps you optimize this advantage.

4. Emotional Intelligence (EIQ)

Emotional intelligence involves recognizing, understanding, and controlling your thoughts, emotions, and behaviors. It plays a crucial role in how we perceive ourselves and interact with others, guiding our personal growth and learning experiences. By setting the right priorities, emotional intelligence influences the majority of our daily decisions and social engagements. The emotional intelligence quotient (EIQ) assessment report introduces the EIQ model and offers personalized development insights across four key areas: self-recognition (SeR), social recognition (SoR), self-management (SeM), and social management (SoM). You can delve deeper into the characteristics and elements that contribute to each measured quotient, gaining valuable knowledge to better understand and manage your EIQ.

Moreover, you can assess your scores in each quotient, discover ways to enhance your performance, and explore tailored developmental tips for each area to optimize your potential. The report also prompts you to reflect on essential aspects of each quotient, helping you to apply your learning effectively and integrate it into your personal growth journey for maximum impact.

I recommend those four assessments, but there are many others as well. Regardless of how many assessments you take, their purpose, especially for *managing up* and advancing your career, is twofold. One is to understand who you are and what your strengths are so you can strategize on the best ways to be invaluable. The second is to understand who you are so you can create productive relationships with your boss and other colleagues.

1. Be Invaluable: Once you identify your strengths, here are some questions to ask yourself:

  I. Am I using my strengths in my current role, and if not, how can I best use them to shine and contribute more in my current role?
  II. How can I find opportunities that align with my strengths and what brings me joy?
  III. What skills can I learn and develop that can complement my strengths and make me invaluable?

Reflecting on these questions and taking action based on your answers will help you be invaluable to the success of your project, your boss, and the organization you work for. Knowing your strengths will help you be so good that they can't ignore you. That will guide the direction your career takes because if you know the specific tasks you're really good at and the areas you have weaknesses in, you'll be able to take opportunities that are right for you.

2. Seek Feedback: In addition to assessments and self-reflection, seeking feedback is a great way to be indispensable to your boss and the organization and to grow as a professional. Professionals who advance in their careers show a genuine interest in their professional development, seek opportunities to learn and grow, and take advantage of training or mentoring programs. By investing in your growth, you become a more valuable asset to your manager and the organization.

In addition to regularly asking for feedback, you have to show your coworkers and peers that you can handle the truth and accept what they have to tell you. A joint study by Wharton School researchers Adam Grant, and Constantinos Vassiliou Coutifaris (experts in organizational behavior, psychology, and management) found that it's not always enough to ask for feedback. Sometimes, you need to show that you can handle the truth. According to the researchers, one way to do this is through self-deprecating humor and criticizing yourself out loud.

3. Provide Regular Updates: There is one unstated rule of *managing up* that professionals who succeed always apply—they keep their boss in the loop. It is important to understand that if you wait to provide an update until you are asked, you have already failed at *managing up*. Keeping your boss in the loop is one of the best things you can do to be invaluable to them. Providing updates is a great way to inform your manager of what's going on so they don't have to micromanage.

Unfortunately, most of us might have experienced micromanagers. Such bosses get anxious because they want to control the project. Providing regular updates without being asked for them will improve your relationships with micromanagers. It will also make you indispensable to any boss and is a strategic way to share your accomplishments and show that you are on top of things.

4. Create Productive Working Relationships with Colleagues and Your Boss: Through increased self-awareness, the results of the assessment will help you to have open communication and create the right environment with your boss or other people in the organization. It starts with you knowing who you are. This will help you identify how your boss and the other people you're interacting with might communicate differently. You can also openly discuss the subject with them. Tell them your communication style and ask them what they prefer. A good practice is to develop a **How to Work With Me** document.

The **How to Work With Me** document lists who you are and provides brief information about you that can be used as a discussion reference with colleagues. This document is critical if you are a manager and can be a discussion reference with your direct reports.

The truth is that everyone is different. For example, you might be the type of person who likes directness in communication and doesn't want to spend time chitchatting. The best thing for you is to stick to business and get things done. Efficiency and effectiveness might be your top priorities. Now, that's great; There's nothing wrong with that. However, not everyone is the same. Your boss might be the type of person who likes to start communication with a personal conversation about something outside of work. On the other hand, you might be the type of person who wants to start with pleasantries, but your boss might want to get directly to the point. Knowing your communication style makes it easier to adapt when you need to so you can get the most out of your communication no matter the situation.

This **How to Work With Me** document can be in any format, and it's important to remember that it's not meant to be sent to your colleagues to ask them to conform to your styles. Rather, it's a discussion point for you to be aware of who you are and a reminder that others are different. The goal is to understand how others operate so you can create a productive working relationship centered around mutual growth that leads to productivity and career development.

Here are the main points to include in the document; however, feel free to add to or remove from what is listed here.

I. **How to Work With Me**
- My communication style: _____
- My leadership style: _____
- How to best interact with me: _____
- How I am as a person: _____
- How I am as a leader: _____

5. Strengthen your relationships by building trust and credibility. Establishing trust is vital in *managing up*. Consistently deliver high-quality work, meet deadlines, and maintain confidentiality. Be honest, reliable, and transparent in your interactions. Building a trustworthy reputation will strengthen your relationship with your manager.

CHAPTER 5

Mobilize Your Boss—Adopt and Align

"Great collaboration feels like playing jazz."
~ Ray Dalio, Principles

The relationship between you and your boss is one of the most important factors when it comes to your career, your energy and life at work, and the impact you make.

Mobilizing your boss is about creating a productive working relationship with them, along with an environment where you collaborate effectively, add value, are recognized for your achievements, and can influence decision-making. Ray Dalio, in his book *Principles*, describes the similarities between collaboration and playing jazz. He states, as in Jazz, great collaboration involves combining different skills like different instruments, improvising creatively, sometimes letting others drive things while other times driving it yourself. It requires listening to the people you are playing with and sometimes subordinating yourself to the goals of the group so as to achieve great results together.

There are four steps to achieving that:

1. Develop a Productive Working Relationship

A great relationship with your boss is nice to have, but having a productive working relationship is a *must* for you to advance in your career, make an impact, and enjoy your work. That's why, to effectively *manage up*, you must prioritize creating a productive working relationship with your boss that is centered on mutual growth and understanding.

A very helpful concept in this area is to understand that while the Golden Rule is to treat and communicate with others the way you want to be treated and communicated with, a better option is the Platinum Rule, which is to treat and communicate with others the way they want to be treated and communicated with. Communicating with your boss the way they want to be communicated with means getting to know them and developing empathy and active listening skills. Developing a productive working relationship also means that not only are you striving to be the best professional you can be and add value to the organization and your team, but at the same time, you are really thinking about how you can be a great follower. This means you will have to shift the focus from yourself to your boss.

You've spent a lot of time in the previous chapters focusing on you, identifying your strengths, vision, goals for your organization and yourself, and what you see for your career and your interests. At this point, the focus should be shifted to your boss. This requires you to have a servant leadership mentality. Instead of thinking, *How can I make my life and my work easy?* You should instead ask, *How can I make my boss's life and work easy? How can I help my boss achieve their goals and projects?* The truth is that your boss will have a bigger picture of your projects, including their goals and why you're working on them, so that shift of focus is going to be helpful.

With that in mind, determine the answers to the following questions:

- How does your boss like to be communicated to?
- How do they like to lead?
- How do they communicate?
- How do they manage projects?
- What are their preferences?

The purpose of getting to know who your boss is and their preferences in terms of communication, management, and leadership is so that you can take proactive measures to create and cultivate a very productive working rapport and relationship with them. If, like you, your boss is able to take a communication or leadership assessment, you can communicate about it and share your results so both of you can find ways to collaborate and communicate more effectively. If your boss hasn't taken an assessment, let them know that you took this one and explain how it would be good for the team to take it as well.

Another option to get to know your boss is to discuss with them the How to Work with Me document you created in Chapter 4. Ask them to share how they prefer to be communicated to and always work with that in mind.

While getting to know your boss, it can be advantageous to create a **How to Best Work with My Boss** document. Here are the main points that you can include in that document; however, feel free to add to or remove from what is listed here.

- What is my boss's communication style?
- What is my boss's leadership style?
- What method of communication does my boss prefer (email, call, walk-in)?
- What type of update does my boss need from me—and how frequently?

2. Perspective Taking: Curiosity over Judgment

There will be days when you see things very differently from how your boss sees them. Seeing things from different perspectives is inevitable. Effectively *managing up* requires one to practice perspective-taking, which prominent psychologist David W. Johnson defined in his 1975 article in the *Journal of Personality and Social Psychology* as: "the ability to understand how a situation appears to another person and how that person is reacting cognitively and emotionally to the situation"[4]

In his book *To Sell Is Human*, Daniel Pink introduces perspective-taking, explaining that it is sort of like empathy but with your brain instead of your heart. It's basically pausing and considering another person's perspective every time you interact with them.

As you can see in the picture, one person is saying the number is six because that's what it looks like from their end, while the other is saying it's nine because that's what they see from their perspective.

---

[4] David W. Johnson, "Cooperativeness and Social Perspective Taking," *Journal of Personality and Social Psychology* (1975).

This image demonstrates what happens when we don't practice perspective-taking; there will be projects in which your boss sees things from a different angle than you. In such cases, you're going to have differences. Those who *manage up* effectively focus on having productive conversations and being curious instead of judging their boss and concluding that they are wrong.

Instead of just assuming that their perspective is the only correct one, those who *manage up* effectively keep an open mind and try to see things from their boss's perspective. Create that productive, curious conversation with your boss so you can both be on the same page.

3. Develop Big-Picture Thinking

In the study that McKinsey & Company conducted, where they interviewed 1,200 marketing leaders, they found that the key determinant of effectively *managing up* was taking on the big issues, those in sync with the boss's agenda and contributing to the company's overall performance. During the study, the marketing leaders were asked about their primary role, and the responses given by the most effective and successful leaders were very different from the rest. While most responded that they "ran the marketing organization" or "led their company's advertising and brand campaigns.," the most effective and successful leaders were more likely to describe their primary role as increasing company growth or better outreach to customers to improve performance.

What about you?

How do you describe what you do? More importantly, are you focused only on your project, unit, or department, or are you focused on the organization and the big picture?

To effectively *manage up*, you need to shift your focus from just you and your work to the bigger picture and the strategic vision of your department, team, boss, and organization. The best way to do that is by always asking yourself, "How is my work contributing to the organization's and my boss's goals?"

Open communication with your boss is another important part of shifting this focus. One-on-one meetings are one of the best ways to do this. In such meetings, you should:

I. Update your boss on what achievements you have made (how you contributed to the overall goals of the project and the boss).

II. Update your boss on how you've worked, what you've worked on, the challenges you faced, and how you solved them. This is also an opportunity to share what you will be working on and ask for help with any roadblocks or challenges you might be facing.

The end of this chapter provides a guide for having effective one-on-one meetings, focusing on the five most crucial conversations you should have during them.

There are different types of one-on-one meetings. Some are specifically focused on the tasks and projects you're working on. These are usually meetings where you discuss what you're working on and what you plan to work on. Now, don't underestimate or hate this type of meeting. It's really not for your boss to micromanage your stuff. Instead, they are a great opportunity for you to share anything related to your work and what you're accomplishing.

Remember: those accomplishments and results don't speak for themselves. Like most other executives, your boss is most likely a busy professional focused on achieving multiple things, so this is your opportunity to highlight your achievements, not in a boastful way, but by sharing the things you're proud of that you've accomplished since the last meeting.

The one-on-one meeting is also an opportunity for you to ask questions and confirm that you are working on the right projects. What do I mean by that? Many professionals spend a lot of time on projects without realizing that they are not that important in terms of the company's overall strategy.

Another type of one-on-one meeting is one focused on you and your career. Most companies and managers would say that the professional should set their own agenda for this type of meeting. The boss is there to just hear you and learn how things are going. Now, this type of one-on-one meeting is an opportunity for you to really get to know your boss well, create a relationship with them, and share your vision of where you want to be. Let's say you are currently an individual contributor, but you have the goal of becoming a manager. It's never too early to share that with your boss so you can plan how to get there.

Most professionals skip these one-on-one meetings. This is one of the biggest mistakes a professional can make because these meetings are opportunities for you to nurture your relationship with your boss, share your achievements, and show that you're making a difference in the organization.

One way to ensure that you're communicating well is to invite your boss to share their preferences about communication. Ask them, "How would you prefer to get updates about projects? Would you rather I share them via report or email or just save them in a folder? What is the best way to communicate with you? What's the best way to bring up a problem that we're facing? Would it be during our meetings or just in conversation?" Again, there's no right or wrong answer.

Creating a follower-leader relationship, where you are focused on being the best leader and follower you can be, is really a matter of understanding how your boss operates, discovering what would make their work easier, and then adapting your style to create a productive work environment.

4. Align Strategic Focus and Priorities

Instead of prioritizing and working on the projects you want, it's more effective to align with what your boss wants. Tell them what you will be focusing on and ask them if there is something else that you should give priority to. This ensures that you're working on the projects and items that your boss prioritizes instead of what you think is a priority. Doing this prevents a lot of misunderstanding because when you work on a project that's a priority, everyone is paying attention to what's happening in that project. This doesn't mean you don't work on other projects as well, but that you prioritize your work based on how it aligns with the company's and boss's strategy.

The easiest thing you can do to facilitate this is to send your boss a regular update. This could be weekly or bi-weekly, though I highly recommend that it be weekly. Send an email with an update on what is happening, what's going on, where you're at, what you have achieved, challenges you might have solved, if there are still pending challenges that you're facing, and how you plan to solve them. Last but not least, ask your boss if there's anything that you need to focus on for the coming week and state what you're planning to work on.

Sending such a simple, to-the-point email on a regular basis can have a huge impact on your career. Ensuring that your boss is updated, letting them know that any problem you are facing is immediately addressed, and requesting help when you need it is a great way to not only communicate effectively with them but also to broadcast your achievements.

In summary, creating a mutually productive working relationship with your boss is going to be helpful not only in advancing your career but also in making your day-to-day work environments much, much, much better. Building a servant leadership mentality, making the shift from focusing on yourself to focusing on your boss and the organization, and asking how you can add and create value for the organization and how you can make your boss's work easier will allow you to create that.

Focusing on the bigger picture and strategic vision is another key aspect of *managing up*. Sometimes, we tend to be too detail-oriented and focused on working on our own projects. While that helps us get things done, your boss might have a bigger picture of which project is more important and which one is not. So, it's really important for you to broaden that vision, focus on the bigger picture, and always communicate with your boss to confirm that you're actually focusing on what's important.

Practice perspective-taking. Try to see things from your boss's perspective. Anytime your boss does something that you don't agree with, or you run into a situation where you do not agree on a specific way to do things, instead of being close-minded and just focusing on doing it the way you want to, be curious, have a conversation with them, and try to really understand where they are coming from. At the end of the day, your job as a follower is to make your boss successful by succeeding in your project. Create a productive working relationship by getting to know your leader's work and communication styles. You already know what your communication style is, so adapt to your boss's style. Then, be intentional about your one-on-one meetings.

Below is a one-on-one meeting guide with a list of questions that you can ask your boss. This is something you can practice, and you can use the five questions for emails as well. You can create an email with a list of those five points and send it once a week to your boss. Again, you might spend 20 to 15 minutes creating that weekly email, but the payoff will be incredible.

One-on-One Meeting Guide: Five Crucial Conversations to Have

- Share your achievements since your last meeting.
- Share challenges you faced and how you overcame/will overcome them.

- Share what you will focus on until your next meeting and confirm that its priority aligns with your boss's.
- Request the help/support you need from your boss.
- Ask how you can help your boss.

CHAPTER 6

Create Your Own Luck—Be at the Right Place at the Right Time

"Luck is what happens when preparation meets opportunity."
~ Seneca, Roman philosopher

If you have already developed a mindset of taking full ownership and have taken ownership of your career, and if, as discussed in the previous chapters, you've already developed self-leadership and have a deep understanding of your boss's communication and leadership style, you have made significant progress toward creating a productive working relationship. Sometimes, though, a productive working relationship with your boss and all of that self-leadership may not get you promoted or to the career path of your dreams.

Well, if you're one of the lucky few, you might have a manager who will be as concerned as you are about your career growth, the alignment of your passion and your work, and so on. Sometimes, though, your boss might be willingly blind to your strengths. The reality is that it's no one's job but your own to ensure your needs are met, that you're in a job that you love, and that your strengths are aligned with your goals and work. The harsh reality is that no one is going to care about your career goals as much as you do.

And that's not bad news, by the way. It's the beginning of empowerment: recognizing that if it's to be, it's up to you. This means you must take ownership. You have to realize that no one is coming to save you, and you have to choose not to leave your fate in the hands of a manager or the company you work with if they are not the type to recognize you. If you do leave it up to them, you're at risk. That's the mindset that professionals who advance in their careers have:

If it's to be, it's up to me.

You might not get the promotion that you've been working towards for years; you might get laid off with no prospect on the horizon, or you might just end up hating your job with no way out. But if you take the "if it's to be, it's up to me" mentality, you're going to do all you can to change that by taking ownership of your career goals and aligning your strengths and passion with what you do to create a better and more lasting impact.

Here are a few strategies you can use to create your own luck.

1. Enhance Your Visibility

Sometimes, you can be doing everything right, adding value to your boss, and contributing as much as you can to the organization, but your boss might simply not believe in you. Unfortunately, cases like this do exist. The sad reality is that only great leaders recognize other great leaders. Only great leaders recognize the strength of people. In situations like this, you have to enhance your visibility within your organization, raise your profile, showcase your talents to senior management, and get the attention of your boss's boss and other executives without going over your boss's head. If you're going to advance in your career and make an impact, you will need to be in front of great leaders so that they, the company's executives, and its stakeholders can see you in action and know about the great work that you do. Just because you're working with a boss who is not willing to see your strengths or who doesn't believe in you doesn't mean that other leaders should not be exposed to your work.

If, unfortunately, your boss is not putting you in front of stakeholders, you will have to find your own platform and ways to be seen. That way, the executives that you look up to, the executives who are in a position to sponsor you and present you with opportunities, get to see you in action. They will get to see the impact that you're making and your strengths, and most of all, they will get to know what you're looking for. That way, when the right opportunity comes along, you will be the person who comes to their mind.

Here are some ways you can be seen by other leaders without going over your boss's head.

2. Celebrate Wins Publicly

We've covered in previous chapters how we need to be aware of our wins and recognize them. Now, I want to cover how celebrating wins can actually help you be seen by the other stakeholders and leaders in the organization. There's one thing that we all have in common, and that is that everyone loves great news. One way to be seen in action is to share good news with all stakeholders, especially when it's time to celebrate wins. If you and your team have achieved something, whether it is increasing revenue, hitting your goal, meeting a deadline, or decreasing costs, it is a perfect opportunity for you to share that achievement by congratulating your team *publicly*. The key term here is "publicly." It could be by sending an email and copying all stakeholders or sharing on an internal social media platform. However you do it, celebrate the wins and achievements publicly.

Fiona is a sales executive who successfully increased her team's sales revenue by 15% more than the predicted growth. Instead of celebrating with her team during her team-members-only meeting, she could send an email, copying her boss, her boss's boss, and other executives, commending her team for the hard work and attention they all gave to making this achievement possible.

Though simple, such an email can have large positive effects. When you copy your boss and your boss's boss or any other leaders in the organization in the email, guess what? They're all going to love it because it's a simple email with congratulatory good news that everyone can celebrate. Not only will it cheer up the executives, but they'll also acknowledge and remember your achievements, even if they may not respond to that email or say something immediately. Celebrate the wins: praise your team in public.

3. Get Involved in Projects or Activities That Show Your Strengths and Passion

The second thing that you can do is prioritize visibility by getting involved in projects or activities that show your strengths and passion. If your boss is not putting you in front of stakeholders, you need to find your own way of doing that. One thing to do is look for cross-functional or internal projects that will involve or be debriefed to stakeholders. If one doesn't exist, guess what? You can propose a project that aligns with the corporate value or vision or that solves a problem/addresses a need.

A client of mine volunteered to start a public speaking group for the sales team of the company she worked with to provide an opportunity for the team to practice and help them with the presentations they make for their clients. This public speaking group ended up being an awesome platform where the sales team bonded; they learned from each other and became a better sales team. My client was commended for it and even got promoted to management. She used her leadership and strategic skills to drive the process and presented the team's findings to the executive team. The CEO recognized the impact and promoted her to lead a special training project for the entire team. Now, this is an example of her creating the role that she wanted and just being visible in that.

4. Create an Opportunity to Get to Know and Communicate with the Leaders You Want to Work With

My client Emmy always dreamed of being part of the finance and merger and acquisition department at the company she worked with. She worked in a different department, but she had the skills and desire to transfer to the finance department. When Emmy learned that the head of the finance department always got to the office at 6:30 a.m., she started going to work at the same time. She caught him in the morning and shared her passion for the work, what she was accomplishing, and what her goals were. Sure enough, when an opportunity opened up in his department, she was the first person to know and apply for that role.

Another option is to attend an optional meeting if the senior executive/s you want to get to know or that you hope will sponsor you or recognize your work will be present. When you go, actively participate so everyone knows what you do and how you can contribute.

That's how you create your own luck: by being seen by the executives or leaders who can sponsor you and present you with opportunities. Create opportunities to communicate with them by turning small talk into meaningful talk. There is a saying: "It's not what you know; it's who you know." Now, I want to challenge that because it's really not who you know. It's actually who knows you. It's not how many people you know; it's how many people know you.

We can even get deeper into challenging this because, at the end of the day, especially when it comes to career networking, it's not really how many people know you as a person. It's how many people know your strengths, how many people know your passion, and how many people know what you're exactly looking for and what you are good at.

The best question to ask to know if you are doing this right is this one: Let's say the people you are networking with or the executives you want to work with are aware of an opportunity that fits what you are looking for and also what you are good at—would you be the first person that comes to their minds?

If the answer is yes, then you are doing a great job of broadcasting your strengths, desires, and goals. If the answer is no, then you will need to do a better job at this.

One way to ensure that people not only know you but actually know what you're good at, what your passion is, or what you're looking for is to find each and every opportunity to turn small talk into meaningful conversations.

Water-cooler conversations are a perfect opportunity to share info about you instead of having a conversation about the weather. A better way to use this opportunity is to actually turn small talk into a meaningful conversation. So, if you have two minutes in the kitchen with someone while getting coffee, instead of just chatting about the weather or just trying to kill that time, as some people would say, you can actually share about the project that you're working on or ask about the projects they are working on. Or you can just share a recent accomplishment you've had, a challenge you're addressing, or what you and your team are working on. That way, that person who just had a two-minute conversation with you knows something meaningful about you, and you also get to know something meaningful about them. Consequently, the next time they think of an opportunity, you'll be the person who comes to their mind.

You might have heard of an elevator pitch. That's a one- to three-minute statement that shares something about you. Now, it doesn't have to be just who you are or what you do. It can be different for different people, but you have to practice sharing a challenge that you're facing or an exciting project that you're working on to take advantage of all of those small-talk opportunities, whether they're in the kitchen as you're getting your coffee or water or warming up your lunch or in an elevator. What is that meaningful conversation that you can have?

"Opportunity dances with those already on the dance floor."
~ H. Jackson Brown, American author

So, that's your way of really being known: showcasing your strengths, goals, and especially what you are looking for so that others remember you. That way, your name will be the first one mentioned when an opportunity arrives that you are the right fit for.

5. Turn Complaints into Opportunities

Mary, one of my clients, was leading a project. With three direct reports, she was tasked with managing the team and completing the training documents for the entire company. Her boss came and further compressed the time so that the deadline was moved up. With the deadline quickly approaching, each team member was working as hard as possible. Mary thought that her boss was pushing her beyond her limits. Everyone on the team was working hard and was exhausted.

Now, Mary had two options in this situation. Option one was to complain: "How can they expect the impossible?" And when the direct reports complained to her, she could have passed the blame by saying, "Well, the big boss wants us to meet this deadline," and complained along with them.

Now, this might have helped her in the short term by allowing her to bond with her direct reports. However, it would have had a negative effect on her career and her direct reports. If all she did was complain, the whole team would be exhausted, burnt out, and lose their excitement. The project might or might not get done, but even if it did, people would dread doing their work. However, Mary had another option: She could proactively study the problem and become part of a solution instead of complaining about it. In this case, that is what Mary did.

First, Mary studied the problem. She stated, "We have a problem: We have to meet this deadline, but we only have three team members at this point, and we have this budget." Then she looked at all of the implications. She set up an appointment with her boss and said, "We have this situation where, if we try to get it done in the time frame that we have, we will have burnt-out employees who are not going to be excited about their work. We might have a decrease in quality because we are rushing to get it done." However, she recommended an alternative solution: "Perhaps we can hire a team member and get this done."

Guess what? Her boss was actually not opposed to that idea because she'd already communicated the implications of hiring a new person, getting them on board, and getting the work done, and she explained how hiring that one person could not only solve the problem but potentially even allow the company to expand and do more things and create more opportunities. That was the solution that she presented, and fortunately, her boss accepted it, and they started hiring.

So, even though Mary and her team were working extremely hard, they came up with a solution. The point is that how you respond to inefficiencies, problems, and bureaucracy in your organization will either make you a great employee or leader or it will make you a disengaged whiner. Professionals who advance in their careers and are recognized for the value they add notice problems and think about how they can create awareness of them, solve them themselves, or empower others to solve them. They choose to be a part of the solution. They have an "if not me, then who" attitude.

Whiners, on the other hand, complain about the problem. They bond with other complainers, and they disengage. They assume that management's intention is to make their work and life harder. So, you, as a professional, have two options. Option one is to complain about the problems, how much the boss makes your life and work harder, and how it's a toxic work environment. Option two is for you to actively notice the problem and create some sort of solution, bringing others along to help—basically, to be a part of the solution.

In this chapter, we looked at three strategies: being seen by others, being known for what you do, and also actively turning complaints or problems into solutions—and being a part of the solution. When you do those three things, you're creating your own luck. That way, when an opportunity comes, you will be right there to reap the benefits.

CHAPTER 7

High-Impact Communication

"If I had more time, I would have written a shorter letter."
~ Blaise Pascal, Lettres Provinciales, 1657

Sam is a middle manager at a tech firm. He has done some research about the company's competitors and is excited to present his findings at one of the upcoming meetings with executives. He is confident that his findings will show the executives that the company needs to make some changes to its sales strategies. Otherwise, it risks losing about 20% of its clients. Sam is excited about the findings and was asked to present at the next meeting, and at least three of the executives he sees as potential sponsors will be there.

Sam arrives at the meeting well-dressed and prepared. When it's his turn to present, he shares his slides and starts talking about the research: the methodology he and his team followed and the type of work they did. Before he can get to the findings, he's interrupted by one of the executives, who says, "Sam, it seems that you guys have done extensive work here. Why don't you discuss this with Lynn (Lynn is Sam's manager) and share your findings with her? Since we only have a few minutes left, perhaps we can finalize the rest of the agenda items quickly."

Sam is crushed. He really can't understand what happened.

The simple communication mistake Sam makes here is actually pretty common in most workplaces. How we communicate can either make or break our careers. The quality of our relationships with our coworkers, the impact we make with them or in the workplace, and whether we influence others or not all depend on how we communicate. Effective communication is one of the most valuable skills you can have, especially when it comes to *managing up*, working with executives, collaborating with other managers, being present, and showcasing your work. It is one of the key skills to develop.

In this chapter, I want to introduce you to a communication method that is extremely useful in the workplace. It is called **BLUF**.

BLUF is a military communication acronym that stands for "Bottom Line Up Front." It is designed to enforce speed and clarity in reports and emails. The basic idea is very simple: put the most important detail, conclusion, or point first. Don't tease or delay your main point because people are busy, and time is valuable.

BLUF can be applied to all types of communication, from simple email exchanges with your coworkers and boss to public speaking, such as presentations.

Now, let's consider Sam's case. When he was giving the presentation to the executives, he started from a logical beginning, and he tried to give the background first. He started by telling them how he and his team had done the research, what kind of methodologies they'd used, and how they collected their data, which is all very good and necessary information but wasn't the main point and was not the conclusion of his findings. Sam mistakenly thought to show them the logical steps that he had taken. However, the executives had the goal of quickly grasping his purpose. When the steps took time, the executives cut him off before he could get to his main point. What could Sam have done differently?

Sam needed to flip that structure. Instead of starting with the methodology, with why and how they had done the research, he could have stated his findings. Imagine if Sam had started by saying, "My team and I found, through our research, that if we as a company don't change our sales strategy, there is a likelihood that we could lose 20% of our clients to our competitors," and then continued by discussing how they had come to that conclusion. I bet the meeting would have gone differently, and I bet the executives would have been curious enough to make time to hear his presentation. Even if they didn't, at least he would have made his main point. In all likelihood, though, everyone would have been excited about his results, and their next logical question would have been, "How did you come up with these findings?" Then, he could have provided more information and gone deeper.

When communicating, you need to flip the structure and put your bottom line up front. You should be able to point to one or two sentences that contain the bottom line of your text or presentation, the conclusion, findings, or recommendations. Once you have, you can add as much backstory as you'd like. That way, if what happened to Sam happens to you, an executive cuts you off and says, "We're going to move on," at least everyone has heard your conclusions.

BLUF is not just an effective communication format for presentations; it can be applied to any communication, especially in the workplace. Just start with the main point and then add as much context as you'd like. So, the next time you're communicating with anyone in the office, remember the acronym BLUF: "Bottom Line Up Front."

The goal is to remember that not everyone has the time to read your entire email or to wait and listen to you until you get to your conclusion. So, instead, start with the main point and then add as much context as you can. Here are several other scenarios where you can apply BLUF.

Let's say you want to communicate with your boss but do not require action from them; it's just an FYI type of email. If so, get right to the point. For example, your email could be,

"Dear (insert boss's name here), we are decreasing the budget for this project to this amount."

That's an FYI. No action is needed from them; they just need to be informed. But don't stop there. You can add as much context and backstory as needed. That way, when your boss receives the email, they will at least know what the main point is, and if they have time and they're interested, they can read the backstory. If they don't, at least you have communicated your most important point.

Let's say you are providing suggestions. Using the BLUF method, you might start with:

- *Dear (insert boss's name here), I suggest we increase the budget for this project from this amount to this amount...*
- *Dear (insert boss's name here), I'm suggesting that we push the deadline for this project from this date to this date...*

In both examples above, you're starting with the main point, the bottom line, the most important thing, but don't stop there because that would leave everyone confused or wanting more information and may lead to needless back-and-forth emails asking for clarifications. Instead, add the backstory and state your thought process. That way, when they get your recommendation, it's not seen as a demand but as a suggestion.

Let's say you have a question. Again, use the BLUF method. Simply ask your question. However, using BLUF doesn't mean just saying the bottom line—it means communicating the bottom line up front. Once you ask your question, it can be interpreted in multiple ways. That's why you need to add your insights or the reason behind your question.

Open with: "Dear (insert boss's name here), I have this question…" Add your question, followed by why you are asking the question and any insights you might have: "I'm asking this question because I'm thinking about how we can improve [X]" or "I have a few suggestions that I want to make, but I first want to know your answer." You're communicating the bottom line upside down, but at least you're sharing your insight and reason for asking, and it's not just a random question. Do the same thing if you encounter a problem: Communicate the problem but also offer a solution and show your thought process.

Again, you're communicating the bottom line up front. You're using the BLUF method. So, you're going to share, "We're facing this and this and this challenge here." But at the same time, if you stop there, it's going to seem like a complaint, or people might not really understand where you're coming from. Communicate the problem, but at the same time, offer a solution and show your thought process. That way, as mentioned in the previous chapter, you're not just stating a problem; you're actually becoming part of the solution.

Let's say you want an action from your boss. Again, start with the action item. You might say, "Hey, boss, I want you to approve this budget for me by Wednesday." Then, add as much context as you would like. You can also say, "We want it by Wednesday because we want to send the data to our client." You can also share why you want the budget increased, why you want it approved, and all of those details. By doing this, you quickly communicate what exactly you need. Your boss knows the bottom line. You're not wasting their time, but you're also offering them details to give them context.

In summary, the BLUF method empowers you to communicate effectively with your boss and coworkers. It ensures that your message is clear and that your audience is informed. When it comes to *managing up* and specifically communicating with your boss or other executives or higher-ups in the organization, there are two key aspects to pay attention to.

I. Always use the BLUF method: Share the bottom line up front.

II. Remember not to just share the bottom line, as this can come off as abrupt and lead to miscommunication, inefficiencies, and unnecessary back-and-forths. In the worst-case scenario, you can be seen as an uncritical thinker. So, with the BLUF method, share the bottom line first, but that's not the only thing you share.

When using the BLUF method, allow the reader to spend as much time as they like on the communication. That way, if they stop at the first sentence, at least they know what you're asking, the point you're making, the conclusion of the finding, or whatever the main idea is. However, it's key to also provide backstories to help them understand where you're coming from.

So, there are two aspects of BLUF that I want to make sure you understand. It's the bottom line first, but at the same time, it's not just the bottom line. You're adding context, offering solutions, and also stating your curiosity to give them enough information if they want or need it.

Specificity

The other aspect of effective communication is being specific. This means not using vague terms like "soon," "later," or "it was great." These terms can mean different things to different people, so being very specific with the words you choose will help you become a better communicator.

The effectiveness of your communication will make or break your career and determine how influential you will be in the organization. Professionals who can gather their thoughts, find the main point, and communicate it effectively are the ones who can easily influence other people.

Public Speaking and Storytelling

The second aspect of communication is public speaking, particularly presenting in meetings and group settings. While the BLUF method is useful for public speaking, as it's all about getting to the main point and conclusion and then presenting other details, there are other tools that you can use to become an effective public speaker and great storyteller.

Public speaking and storytelling are beyond the scope of this book. However, I want to mention here that these two communication skills are key to helping you mobilize your boss and industry peers. You can join organizations like Toastmasters to practice and become better at public speaking and leadership. Several AI tools can also help you become a better speaker. Yoodli, an AI-based communication coach, is one that I recommend. It not only helps with public speaking but also other aspects of communication, such as impromptu communication and storytelling.

Effective communication is one of the key skills to *managing up* because how you are seen and how well you communicate affect how influential you are.

CHAPTER 8

Develop Strong Support and a Network of Thought Partners

"If you want to go fast, go alone. If you want to go far, go together."
~ African Proverb

In the previous chapters, we talked about you fully understanding what *managing up* is and what it is not and identifying what gets in your way and addressing that. Then we got into the actual work of embracing *managing up* and understanding that it benefits your boss and the organization as much as it benefits you, that it is a "win-win." You've also identified your strengths and weaknesses, have a deeper understanding of yourself, are working productively with your boss, and are improving your communication skills. All that is going to make you one of the superstars in the company. This chapter is about elevating the game so that, as the CEO of your career, you can develop thought partners within the organization and industry-wide to advance your career.

Before we discuss the three best practices to get there, I encourage you to revisit the exercise you completed in Chapter 2, where you created your network map, and take some time to reflect. How can you intentionally build your network of connections? How can you nurture those relationships and ensure they align with your core values, your *why*, and your career goals? Reflect on the questions and your networking map as you explore the following three best practices.

1. Act within Your Unit, but Think Organization- and Industry-Wide

Managing up is not just about your boss or your boss's boss. You have to think about your peers within the organization and also within your industry because it really is about expanding your reach, creating impact, and being known in your industry and community for what it is that you do and contribute. Most professionals, even when they're really successful, are sometimes so concerned with being the best employee they can be and building relationships with their supervisor and subordinates, if any, that they forget to build relationships with their peers and outside of their organization within the industry.

I often hear managers say, "It's lonely at the top." They lose their friends within the company once they become a manager to their peers, and they feel lost. That is because they're only thinking about their role within the organization. Professionals who succeed act within their unit but think organization- and industry-wide. With this big-picture thinking, you create collaboration and relationships with your peers without going above your boss's head. You can create relationships with other departments, managers, or people who are at your level elsewhere in the company, understanding what they're going through, the projects they're working on, and the challenges they're facing. This gives you a broader perspective of the work you do within your department.

2. Collaborate and Share

A great way to create, build, and nurture relationships is through collaboration, sharing, serving, and giving. People often think about networking or finding relationships with the idea of getting something from the people they network with, which usually backfires. This chapter shares the perspective that networking is about sharing, giving, and collaborating. When you come together with others, you create synergy and can achieve more with others than you can on your own.

The benefit of having a great relationship with peers in your organization is that it gives you thought partners and people to share best practices with, people who understand the culture of the company but, at the same time, are far removed from your department and are not necessarily working with the people you work with. They can give you a different perspective; they can be your sounding board and add value to you.

Sharing valuable resources and adding value to the industry and peers also helps you become known in the industry for what you do in your company. You can share your knowledge, an article or a video you found beneficial, or actively serve as a volunteer in industry-wide organizations. When you're known and valued in your industry, your company will see that. You're creating a brand for yourself, and people will come to your company because of you. That makes you invaluable both within and outside of your organization.

When you add value to the organization and the industry, and when you have visibility outside of your organization, the people in your organization will value you more. Corporate leaders notice who is visible to customers, stakeholders, and the broader industry. So, if you were to contribute an article and it was to go viral, reach clients, or even just add value, people would begin to know you and, by association, your organization. That is adding value to the company in a different way. Additionally, if you join an industry-wide association and volunteer, for example, as a board member, that recognition can significantly enhance your value and benefit your organization.

3. Create Thought Partners and See Ways to Add Value

Developing a network of thought partners, again, aligns with what was stated in previous chapters. You must actively create a practice, routine, and system to create and maintain these relationships. One really good practice is to have a fixed once-a-month coffee or lunch hour where you would have a conversation with a person that you haven't met before. I understand that this can be uncomfortable, but growth can feel that way when we are in a comfort zone. By meeting new people, you can generate new ideas, increase collaboration, and expand your relationship network.

This chapter is about elevating your game and expanding your value to the industry.

When you add value to the industry, the industry will recognize you. That outside recognition, in turn, creates better recognition within your company. Expanding your reach and having those connections outside of your industry is a great resource—for you and, of course, for them.

Conclusion

"The best way to predict the future is to create it."
~ Anonymous

You are the CEO of your career. This means that creating that ideal future will require you to have a strong vision of where you want to go, take 100% ownership, and have a methodical approach to getting there. *Managing up* is about managing all of the resources you have to create a conducive environment and a productive working relationship with your boss so you can add value to them, the organization, and yourself and advance in your career. Effectively *managing up* requires a full understanding of what it is and what it is not and conviction as to why you want to do it. The next step is understanding what stands in your way and spending time unlearning the myths associated with *managing up* and all of the other things that we naively believe.

It's also critical to understand that:
- **Results do not speak for themselves.**
    - Numbers, impressions, and key performance indicators are great ways for companies to track and measure performance. However, those numbers don't speak for

themselves. You are responsible for sharing the successes, the numbers, and the results you are getting.

- **You do not get what you deserve or what you're worth. You get what you ask for.**
  - This is just as true in your professional life as it is in your personal life. You don't get what you deserve or are worth; you get what you ask for and, most importantly, what you settle for. So, here's a question for you. What are you settling for? And what are you asking for? Are you really asking what you want, or are you just settling for what you've got?

- **It's not just how much value you're adding.**
  - Yes, any professional is going to want to add value to the company, which is great. However, it's not really how much value you add. It's how much value company leaders think you add. So, if you're at a company and you think you're adding value, but your company does not, there's some misalignment. At the end of the day, you could be adding value but not getting anything in return. The reason for this is that it's not just adding value; it's making sure that the people above you understand that you're adding value.

- **Your boss is too busy to notice your work.**
  - Help yourself by helping them see your accomplishments.

- **Great bosses and managers are nice to have, but if you really want to be successful, your success should not depend on it.**
  - A great working relationship with your boss is something that you can create, even when you have a bad or difficult

boss. Professionals who succeed believe that a productive relationship with the boss is not something they expect but one that they create and cultivate.

- **Only great leaders recognize leaders.**
    - Unfortunately, your boss might not recognize or appreciate your work or your strengths. Even worse, they may not believe in you. This could be either intentional or unintentional. Either way, it's your responsibility to be proactive and find opportunities to be around those who will recognize and value your skills and strengths.
- **It is not how many people you know or how many people know you.**
    - It's how many people know your passions, how many people know your strengths, or how many people know your interests. A great question to ask here is, "If someone is talking to one of your professional connections about an opportunity that you are the perfect fit for and that you're also interested in, would that professional connection think of you immediately? If the answer is yes, you have networked effectively. When you network effectively, you will be the first person your connections think of when opportunities arise, so that's a key measure for you here.
- **Your ego is what stands in the way.**
    - You soar and thrive when you stop thinking about yourself. I learned this the hard way. Anytime you're insecure, feel like you're an imposter, or are doubting yourself, your beliefs, or your strengths, guess what? You are thinking about yourself. The easiest way to stop this is to remind

yourself of the purpose of what you're doing and how you're doing something greater than yourself. When your focus shifts from you to the purpose, you're going to forget your insecurities.
- **Imposter syndrome is real, so overcome it.**
- **Communication is the magic tool.**
    - Your ability to adapt to others' way of communication and to see things from their perspective will take you places. If there's one skill that you should never stop learning and improving, it's communication. Whether it's talking face-to-face with your colleagues, writing emails, messages, and texts, or speaking in public, improving the way you communicate will reward you in multiple ways. Any investment in this area will give you high returns.
- **Self-knowledge does not stop.**
    - The more you're aware of your strengths, weaknesses, communication style, and preferences, the more emotionally intelligent you become and the easier it gets to understand others. When you lead from that perspective and take the time to understand other people and their preferences, you create a conducive environment that allows you to grow. What you've done will make you great and help you be the CEO of your career, but you must realize that you can't get there on your own.
- **You can't make it on your own. You need thought partners**
    - Create thought partners and people in the industry to grow with, people for whom you care about giving as much as you do about getting. This world is really about you doing

other things with others, collectively helping each other and growing.

- **Care about giving as much as you can to the industry.**
    - See ways you can add value, not just for your company and your boss but to the industry and beyond. When you give value to your industry, you create opportunities for the value to come back to you. It's not just about shining within your organization but expanding that light into the industry and making sure that you're creating a community of thought partners.

Gratitude

As I mentioned at the beginning of the book, the insights I've shared helped me chart my own career path. I am incredibly grateful that you have read this book and started the journey of being the CEO of your career. I hope that this book has given you the tools and concepts, but mostly the mindset, to achieve career success and that you continue to apply these practices and share and collaborate with others on a similar path.

The Art of Managing Up Score Interpretations

Disclaimer: This assessment is not intended to provide a psychological or psychiatric diagnosis, and your completion of the test does not indicate a professional counseling or coaching relationship with the creators or administrators of the test.

Total Score 105-155

This score indicates that you are not *managing up* at all. You may not have a great and productive working relationship with your boss, feel appreciated, recognized, and compensated for the value you bring to the organization, have been passed over for opportunities that are right for you, or have let frustration or resentment build up. Your score indicates that you may have to actively work on this skill, learn the art of *managing up*, demystify the myths associated with managing up, and develop your ability to *manage up* by working with a coach or through other means. Actively *managing up* not only gives you agency but allows you to create a productive, win-win environment that contributes significantly to your overall satisfaction at work.

As you read the book, create a step-by-step plan to develop the right understanding of *managing up*, identify what is standing in your way, and address the unique challenges you may be facing, one at a time.

Total Score 55-104

This score indicates that you are somehow *managing up* well but not to your full potential.

While you may be happy with some aspects of your career—for example, you may have a productive relationship with your boss but don't feel appreciated as much, or you may be happy with your compensation plan but unable to influence decision-making.

Overall, your score indicates that you have the potential to master this skill, accelerate your career, and grow both professionally and financially. Since your score falls in the mid-range, you will greatly benefit from all the chapters in this book, answering the reflection questions, and developing an action plan to address your unique skill gaps. Each section of the assessment represents one of the core aspects of *managing up*, such as understanding the concept, demonstrating high levels of self-leadership and self-knowledge, engaging in high-impact communication, mobilizing your boss, and building the right network. The chapters and reflection questions will help you gain clarity on the unique challenges you may be facing and identify key action steps to accelerate your career.

Total Score 0-54

Your score indicates that you are *managing up* well. You may have a productive working relationship with your boss, and you may feel appreciated and well-compensated for your efforts and the value you add. Your score indicates that you know the definition of *managing up* and do not believe in the myths associated with it. You seem to enjoy a great working environment and to be appreciated and recognized.

An ideal score for *managing up* is 31. Depending on how close your score is to that ideal number, you may have mastered this skill. The mistake most individuals make at this stage is that they stop seeing the need to *manage up*, thinking they have already achieved what they need. We recommend that you continue doing what you are doing.

THANK YOU FOR READING MY BOOK!

Just to say thanks for buying and reading my book, I would like to give you a free strategy call with me, no strings attached!

Scan the QR Code:

I appreciate your interest in my book and value your feedback as it helps me improve future versions of this book. I would appreciate it if you could leave your invaluable review on Amazon.com with your feedback. Thank you!

www.ingramcontent.com/pod-product-compliance
Lightning Source LLC
Chambersburg PA
CBHW030242010526
44107CB00030B/1305/J